SIX MONTHS IN BRITISH BURMAH

SIX MONTHS IN BRITISH BURMAH

OR INDIA BEYOND THE GANGES IN 1857

CHRISTOPHER T. WINTER

GYAN

Published by

Gyan Publishing House
5, Ansari Road
Daryaganj, New Delhi-110002
Phone: 011-47034999, 9811692060
E-mail: books@gyanbooks.com

Distribution Network
gyanbooks.com
India, USA, Canada, UK, Australia

ISBN: 978-93-7447-569-0 (PB)

First Published, 1858

2nd Impression 2025

Printed at: Gyan Press, Delhi.

SIX MONTHS IN BRITISH BURMAH
Author: CHRISTOPHER T. WINTER

Front.

Interior of a Burman Temple, Malay Street, Maulmain.

SIX MONTHS

IN

BRITISH BURMAH:

OR,

INDIA BEYOND THE GANGES

IN 1857.

BY CHRISTOPHER T. WINTER.

RICHARD BENTLEY,
NEW BURLINGTON STREET.
Publisher in Ordinary to Her Majesty.

1858.

CONTENTS.

PREFACE.

The following pages are the result of a six-months' residence in the countries of which they treat. During that time I made the people—their manners, customs, institutions, and religion—my particular study. I wandered, sketch-book in hand, amongst the pagodas and temples, and joined the natives in their festivals and amusements as far as a looker-on can be said to do so. I also obtained much valuable information from gentlemen long resident in the country, whose ability to contribute important information was only equalled by their readiness to communicate the result of their experience.

I would express a hope that, at a time

when information respecting our Eastern dominions has received additional interest from late events, the accompanying sketch of British Burmah will not prove unacceptable, and may contribute its mite towards the diffusion of accurate knowledge of that part of our East Indian possessions.

I should also mention that these recollections have been written during the confusion and interruptions incident to a sea-voyage; and I trust that this may be some excuse for the many shortcomings that the intelligent reader will doubtless discover.

C. T. W.

August 1858.

SIX MONTHS

IN

BRITISH BURMAH.

CHAPTER I.

Glance at Calcutta—Ackyab—Rangoon—Shoay Dagon Pagoda—The Great Bell of Rangoon.

I HAD glanced at Calcutta, and looked with no little interest on the motley population, and the many curious sights and sounds of that "city of palaces:" its stately buildings and flat-roofed luxurious houses, in which punkahs make a perpetual breeze, and in which etiolated ladies recline in darkened rooms, and are waited on by obsequious domestics, ever ready to answer the oft-repeated "*qui hy?*" its gay court and esplanade thronged by innumerable carriages, where the governor of millions of people, military celebrities, ci-devant native kings and princes, pensioned rajahs, rich native gentlemen, the sallow-complexioned old Indian, the youth fresh from England destined, according to Macaulay, to make a fortune or die of the liver-complaint, the fair English maiden and troops of European children with their dusky ayahs—all meet to listen to the military music, to enjoy the cool breeze and shades of evening, to see and to be seen. But the heat at this season of the year (the middle of April) is very oppressive in Calcutta even to the acclimated, whilst to the newly-arrived it is almost unsupportable. I was glad therefore to escape to Burmah—a country which, though nearer the line, is more healthy in climate, bolder and more diversified in scenery, and where the heat is tempered by refreshing breezes. It was a country, too, that I had already studied at a distance, and I wished to test my book-knowledge by actual experience. I embarked accordingly on board the steamer "Cape of Good Hope," bound for Ackyab, Rangoon, and Maulmain. Just before weighing anchor, the Hooghly was so obliging as to afford us a capital view of that wonderful tidal phenomenon known by the name of "the Bore," and its effect was illustrated by an unfortunate native boat which, presenting its bow at right-angles to the advancing wave, essayed to ride over the roaring water; but, as if to punish its temerity, it was tossed over like a nut-shell, and a moment after it was floating keel upwards, whilst its previous occupants were swimming with all speed towards the land. We quickly passed the flat but luxuriant shores of the muddy river, and gained the waters of the Bay of Bengal, which are also tinged for miles by the detritus brought down by the Ganges. This has been estimated by one of our first geologists as daily equal in bulk in the flood season to the largest of the Egyptian pyramids.

It was now an interesting study to the ethnologist to observe the different varieties of the human race included amongst our passengers. There was the "mild Hindoo" from the burning plains of Bengal; Madrassees, useful as domestic servants and valets; Eurasians, or country-born half-castes; Chinamen, who in many Eastern countries, as shopkeepers and artizans, supplant to a great extent the more indolent natives; Burmans from the jungles of Ava; Mhugs from the mountainous districts of Arracan. To these may be added our cabin passengers: British officers, civil servants of the East India Company, merchants, American missionaries, and Italian Catholic priests.

On the 29th of April, about twenty hours after leaving Calcutta, we entered the pretty harbour of Ackyab. The light-house is picturesquely situated on a rocky islet, and the land-locked harbour is surrounded by a bold and well-wooded country. Here and there a bungalow, in which the European vegetates and sighs for his native land, peeps out from some shady retreat. The roads are good and planted with umbrageous trees.

At six a.m. on the morning of the 2nd of May we entered the Rangoon river; one of the many branches by which the Irrawaddy —the great highway into the dominions of his golden-footed majesty of Burmah— empties itself into the sea. There on the left we noted the spot where the British forces landed at the commencement of the late war, and further up the river is a sacred grove where, according to the Burman sages, the next Boodh is to appear in about one thousand years. That object in the distance, glittering like a mass of gold amid the green foliage, is the richly-gilded Syriam pagoda. Here and there Burman villages may be seen on the river's bank.

At length the great pile of the Shoay Dagon pagoda looms into view, looking like the giant guardian of the country. It is situated in north latitude 16° 47′, east longitude 96° 13′, and is no less celebrated for its antiquity and vastness than for its importance in time of war, when it is used as a fort. Rangoon, the town adjacent, was founded or rebuilt by the great Alompra, the Burman conqueror, in 1755, and named by him "peace effected," or according to some "victory achieved," in commemoration of his conquests. In a commercial point of view it is the most important town of Pegu, and, before the late war, of the whole Burman empire. Built on the left bank of the eastern branch of the Irrawaddy, twenty-six miles from the sea, and possessing a continuous water communication with the upper provinces, its situation is most convenient for foreign trade. Rafts of valuable teak timber are floated down from the vast forests of Pegu and the mountainous districts of Ava. It presents great facilities for ship-building, which, indeed, has been carried on here since the year 1786. At spring tides the water rises twenty-one feet, and at neaps fifteen feet. The variation of the compass at Rangoon is 2° 48′ easterly.* The native town is

* It is the same at Maulmain.

of a very mean appearance, the houses being made chiefly of bamboo and the leaf of the water-palm; but wood and tiles are being introduced for roofing. Just previous to my visit a most destructive fire had consumed whole streets and bazaars, but they had grown up again like so many mushrooms with astonishing rapidity. A great change has taken place in Rangoon since it has come under the dominion of the British, and large sums of money (more than eleven lakhs of rupees on the city, and about a lakh and a half on the cantonments) have been expended on its improvement. Capital roads and streets now intersect every part of the town, and mostly derive their names from their respective breadths. Many good and spacious "*puckah*" houses, buildings of brick or stone, have been erected, most of which are occupied by mercantile firms. Their gains are often large; but they not unfrequently pay as high as three per cent. a month for money accommodation, so that here, and also at Maulmain (where the rates of interest are equally high) money-lending or private banking is a most profitable business, as good security can generally be obtained.

The most interesting object at Rangoon to the traveller is the great Shoay Dagon or Golden Dagon pagoda before alluded to, and I did not fail to pay a visit to this sacred shrine of the Burman, the holy sepulchre of the devout Boodhist. The foundation is said to have been laid two thousand three hundred years ago. It lies about two miles north of the town, and is built on ground that rises gradually from the river-side till it attains a height of seventy or eighty feet above its previous level. The pagoda is a stupendous mass of solid masonry; it stands on two terraces which face the four cardinal points. The upper one is 900 feet long and 685 feet broad; the base of the building is octagonal, with a circumference of 1355 feet. The area on which it stands is 800 feet square, and is accessible on each side by stone steps, at the side of which are placed enormous griffins; the whole structure gradually tapers to a spire, which is surmounted by the sacred Tee, a cap or crown of open iron-work twenty-six feet high, and hung round with little bells. It is one dazzling blaze of gold, and altogether forms a most magnificent object, its magnitude and massiveness being very remarkable; and it uprears its lofty height from clusters of beautiful mango, cocoa-nut, and other Eastern trees. It is said to contain gold equal in weight to the body of a late Burman king. This celebrated pagoda derives its peculiar sanctity, however, from being the depository, according to Burman tradition, of relics of the last four Boodhs, viz. the staff of Kan-tha-than, the water-dipper of Gau-na-gon, a garment of Ka-tha-pa, and eight hairs from the head of Gau-da-ma! Burman pagodas are not temples, but monuments erected to the memory of Gau-da-ma, and are supposed to contain sacred relics; they are consequently objects of worship to the Boodhist. All of them are built pretty much on the same plan, though varying in detail; the base consists of one or more quadrangles, succeeded by a tapering bell-shaped structure, either round or forming a polygon, the apex of which is crowned with the Tee or umbrella, and without that addition it would be considered incomplete. The building itself is invariably a solid mass of masonry constructed of bricks burnt in the sun, with an outer coating of plaster. In the rainy season many of these pagodas are nearly covered with ferns and other forms of vegetable life; nor is this confined to the old and ruinous, for my attention has often been arrested by those in the course of erection, and I have observed with astonishment a singular proof of the dampness of the climate, viz. that the unplastered bricks have been rapidly covered with luxuriant vegetation, which the builder leaves undisturbed till the return of the dry season, when he can complete his labours.

The Golden Pagoda of Rangoon is surrounded by numerous image-houses containing colossal idols of Gau-da-ma richly gilt; indeed the quantity of gold expended on these religious edifices is something enormous. Not the least remarkable object in the immediate neighbourhood of this pagoda is the great bell of Rangoon, under which I was able to stand upright with ease. It has an inscription in the Burman character, cut in twelve lines of large letters round its circumference, which has been translated by the Rev. G. H. Hough. The concluding words are as follows: "For this meritorious gift, replete with the virtue of beneficence, may he (the king who presented the bell) be conducted to Nieban, and obtain the destined blessing of Men, Nats, and Brahmas by means of divine perfection. May he obtain in his transmigrations only the regal state among Men and Nats. May he have a pleasant voice, a voice heard at whatever place desired, like the voice of Kuthameng Ponnoka and Alamaka, when he speaks to terrify, and like the melodious voice of Karaweik, king of birds, when he speaks on subjects which Nats and Brahmas delight to hear. Whatever may be his desire or the thought of his heart merely, let that desire be fulfilled. Let him not in the least meet with that towards which he has no mental disposition, and for which he has no desire. When the deity Arimadeya* shall be revealed, let him have the revelation, that he may become Withadi Nat, supreme of the three rational existences. In every state of existence let him continually and truly possess the excellence of wisdom, and according to his desire in practices pertaining to this world, and to the divine state, so let it be accomplished. Thus, in order to cause the voice of homage during the period of five hundred years to be heard at the monument of the divine hair in the city of Rangoon, let the reward of the great merit of giving the great bell called Maha Ganda be unto the royal mother queen, the royal father proprietor of life, lord of the white elephant, the royal grandfather Aloungmeng, the royal

* The fifth Boodh, and next to Gaudăma, the last; whose images are now worshipped. Arimadeya is now supposed to be in one of the regions of the Nats.

uncle, the royal aunt queen, the royal sons, the royal daughters, the royal relatives, the royal concubines, the noblemen, the military officers, and teachers. Let the Nats who guard the religious dispensation five thousand years; the Nats who guard the royal city, palace, and umbrella; the Nats who all around guard the empire, the provinces, and villages; the Nats who guard the monuments of the divine hair, around the hill Tampakokta, together with the Nats governing Bomma and Akatha, and all rational beings throughout the universe, utter praises and accept the supplications."

An attempt was made to remove this bell on board a British ship during the war of 1824, but it accidentally fell into the river, and after remaining at the bottom several months it was taken up and restored to its former place. The Soolay pagoda at Rangoon is small but very beautiful, being richly ornamented with green and gold.

CHAPTER II.

The Province of Pegu—Its Area and Fiscal Divisions—The Irrawaddy—The Inhabitants of Pegu—The Administration of the Province—Revenue and Expenditure.

The province of Pegu was added to the British Empire in the East at the close of the last war with the king of Burmah, as is pretty generally known. It lies between the parallels of 15° 44′ and 19° 27′ north latitude, and the meridians of 94° 13′ and 96° 52′ east longitude. Its area is estimated at 32,250 square miles.

It is divided for fiscal purposes into the following divisions:

Rangoon	9,800	square	miles.
Bassein	8,900	„	„
Prome	5,500	„	„
Henzada	2,200	„	„
Tharawaddy	1,950	„	„
Tounghoo	3,900	„	„

The principal river of Pegu is the celebrated Irrawaddy, which has its source in 28° north latitude and 97° 30′ east longitude, and after a course of 900 miles it discharges itself into the sea by nine different mouths; but besides these there are many branches connected with it. In March the river begins to rise, and gradually increases in volume till its waters are forty feet above their lowest level. They rapidly subside in October, when the rains cease and the north-east monsoon sets in.

The inhabitants consist principally of Burmans and Peguans, between whom the stranger cannot distinguish any difference; the Karens, who live in wild and remote districts; the Karen-nee, or red Karens; the Khyins, whose women tatoo their faces; the Yeh-baings, of the Yoma range; and the Shans, who form separate communities.

The administration of the province is entrusted to a Commissioner from the supreme government. The other officers administering civil justice are Deputy-commissioners,

Assistant-commissioners, and Myo-okes. These will be described in a subsequent chapter when treating of the Tenasserim provinces. The Bengal criminal code is the chief authority in the courts, but in the seaport towns commercial transactions are regulated by the English law.

Under the rule of the Burman king the revenue of Pegu is supposed to have been about rupees 15,71,498; but the present revenue amounts to rupees 30,21,062, or upwards of thirty lakhs of rupees. It is raised as follows:

	* Rupees.	Annas.	Pic.
Land	935,988	7	5½
Capitation tax	736,688	14	5
Fisheries	272,036	10	0
Salt	49,715	8	0
Forest produce	1,650	0	0

* In British Burmah accounts are kept in the same way as in India, viz., in Company's rupees, annas, and pie: 16 annas going to the rupee, and 12 pie to the anna. The coins are—rupees, half and quarter rupees, in silver; and in copper quarter-annas and a few smaller copper coins, all of which go by the name of pice.

	Rupees.	Annas.	Pie.
Excise	176,530	10	3
Sea customs	170,927	8	2
Inland customs . . .	391,888	13	4
Municipal tax . . .	30,878	7	0
Port dues	27,501	3	0
Rent on building-lots, town of Rangoon	9,869	0	0
Timber revenue . . .	80,593	14	9
Judicial fines and fees . .	74,313	10	0
Sale of unclaimed property .	11,197	9	11
Bazaar rent. . . .	15,233	15	5
Ferries	933	8	0
Postage stamps . . .	11,750	6	3
Miscellaneous . . .	23,364	5	9¾
	30,21,062	7	9¼

Rupees 17,01,181 is estimated as the civil expenditure of the province, and the census returns give a population of 582,258 souls. It will probably much increase under the present rule, as in other parts of British Burmah.

The American missionaries have established many normal schools, particularly in the Bassein district. A flotilla of steamers keeps up the communication on the Irrawaddy, and several public works are in progress. Rice and teak timber are the principal exports. Agriculture is as yet carried on in a very rude and imperfect manner; but with a settled government this as well as other departments of industry will take a rapid stride.

Slavery has been abolished, and every one will now enjoy the legitimate fruits of his labour. The people are beginning to believe in the permanency of British rule, which, recollecting the abandonment of the province in 1826, they for some time doubted.

CHAPTER III.

The Tenasserim Provinces—Amherst—Approach to Maulmain—Timber-yards and Elephants—Pagoda-crowned Hills—Sketch of Maulmain—Holy Poles or Burman Flagstaffs.

On the 4th of May we left Rangoon for Maulmain, the principal town and port of the Tenasserim provinces; under which name is included the whole of British Burmah south of the newly acquired province of Martaban. This narrow strip of land is about five hundred miles in length, with a varying breadth of from forty to eighty miles. It extends from the point of the junction of the Thoung-yeen river with the Salween on the north, to the Pâk-chan river on the south. On the east it is separated from Siam by a range of mountains, a spur of the Himmalaya, which runs through the whole of the Malay peninsula, and on the west it is washed by the ocean. This tract of country, which, together with Arracan and a part of Martaban, was ceded to the East India Company by the treaty of Yandaboo on the 24th of February, 1826, is divided into three provinces, viz. Maulmain or Amherst province, the chief civil and military station, Tavoy, and Mergui. The rivers most worthy of note are the Salween, Gyne, Attaran, Yé, Tavoy, and Tenasserim. And now, as the traveller approaches this part of Burmah, he is struck by the contrast it exhibits to the low-lying banks of the Hooghly, the flat level land of Bengal, and even to the country in the vicinity of Rangoon. Here is scenery the boldest and most picturesque. Thickly-wooded hills and cloud-capped mountains are the leading features of the landscape. But here before us is Amherst, situated at the mouth of the Salween river in north latitude 16° 15′, and east longitude 97° 34′, at the distance of about twenty-seven miles from

Maulmain by the river. By land the distance is less; there is no road however practicable for carriages or even for horses, but merely a track holding its course through swamps and over rugged hills. Intelligence of importance may be carried to head quarters by means of runners, who can traverse this footpath with little difficulty. Mrs. Judson's lonely grave, under the shadow of a hopea tree, could be discerned from the deck of the vessel. Amherst was so called in compliment to Lord Amherst, who was Governor-General of India when the settlement was formed immediately after the annexation of the country. It was indeed chosen for the capital of the Tenasserim provinces, but, as it proved to be wanting in many of the requisites for a place of such consequence, the seat of government was removed to Maulmain. Amherst now derives its importance from being the pilot station. It is also valuable on account of the salubrity of its climate, and is therefore much resorted to by the residents of Maulmain, who come here for the benefit of sea-air and sea-bathing, particularly during the hot months of February, March, and April.

A run of a few hours up the river brings us to the important town of Maulmain, situated at the junction of the rivers Salween, Gyne, and Attaran, in latitude 16° 29′ north, and longitude 97° 38′ east. It is reckoned one of the healthiest stations in the East. Approaching Maulmain from the Salween, the appearance of the town is rather mean; the banks of the river being occupied by a succession of timber-yards and low thatched sheds; but their importance in connexion with the trade of the place makes ample amends for their somewhat unsightly appearance. In these yards the traveller will see thousands of logs of valuable teak timber, for the export of which Maulmain is famed. Sawyers will be observed busy at work, squaring the logs and making them ready for shipment to the home market. Here, too, the stranger will find illustrated in a wonderful manner the usefulness, power, sagacity, and docility of the elephant; indeed, without its valuable assistance the teak-forests of Burmah could hardly be made available. Each yard has at least two elephants with their respective mahouts, grass-cutters, and keepers. They drag up immense logs of timber from the river's edge to any place desired, and with their tusks, trunk, and feet they shift and stack them according to the will of the mahout, who sits on the animal's neck and directs its movements by means of an iron hook he holds in his hand, and also by his feet and voice. These elephants are worth from four hundred to nine hundred rupees each, according to their size, disposition, and capabilities. Vessels of any tonnage can be towed up to Maulmain by steamer at the spring-tides. The rise and fall of the water is at that time from twenty-one to twenty-three feet.

Although the appearance of Maulmain from the Salween is somewhat spoilt by shabby buildings on the banks of the river, the lover of the picturesque cannot fail to be pleased with the fine range of pagoda-crowned hills that backs the town and runs parallel with it. On these heights many a golden spire flashes in the sun, and grotesque-looking buildings, filled with uncouth idols, arrest the attention of the wanderer at every step, telling of a heathen people and a distant land. Here, too, are built many pretty residences commanding a fine view of the town, river, and adjacent country. Of these the commissioner's is the most conspicuous, its white walls contrasting strongly with the bright green foliage by which it is surrounded. But, proudly towering above every thing else on the range of hills of which I have been speaking, stands the great pagoda. The gaol too is a conspicuous object, behind which numerous small pagodas are visible. Several many-roofed temples may also be observed, and Burman flagstaffs (which have a religious significance and are sometimes called "Holy Poles") are planted at various ditances along the hills. Each one is crowned, like a pagoda, with a *tee* of suitable size, and a few feet from the top is a rude representation of a cock, that bird being the national emblem of the Burmans. These poles are always found in the neighbourhood of religious edifices.

CHAPTER IV.

View from the Great Pagoda—The Great Pagoda and Temples—Inscription on the Great Bell—The Two Classes of Religious Edifices—Sketch of the Exterior of a Boodhist Temple—Interior of the same—Characteristics of the Burman Religion—Description of Maulmain—Population of the Tenasserim Provinces—Unroofing of the Houses at Maulmain.

If the stranger climbs the hill on which the great pagoda is situated, he will be rewarded by one of the most extensive views in the world. "An unbroken range of primitive mountains, four or five thousand feet high," observes Mason, "are seen on the verge of the eastern horizon sweeping around to the north-west like an amphitheatre, where they are lost in the misty distance. From Martaban another range extends directly north, parallel with the west bank of the Salween." Between these is an immense alluvial plain, in the midst of which rises a pile of the most picturesque mountain limestone, cut into many a fantastic shape. One high peak, familiarly known as the "Duke of York's Nose," is discernible from the river below Maulmain. These ranges of rocks and mountains, the intervening plain threaded with several silver rivers, Martaban town with its many spires, all lie mapped out before the spectator standing at the base of the great pagoda. It is a view he will not easily forget; nor can he fail to be astonished at the indefatigable Burman who conveys such masses of materials to the tops of the highest hills, and there erects the gigantic monuments of his faith; indeed, the objects close at hand will arrest his attention more, perhaps, than those at a distance. The pagoda, though much less striking than the Shoay Dagon of Rangoon, is still sufficiently remarkable. The spire is richly gilt, and may be seen at a great distance reflecting the rays of the rising or setting sun. A vault beneath is said to contain one of the hairs from the head of Gau-da-ma, the last Boodh.

It is esteemed a very ancient and sacred shrine by the Burmans. The image-houses or temples around contain many colossal idols, some of which are entirely covered with gold leaf. There is likewise a great bell suspended in the usual way between two posts. It has an inscription in the Burman character; and immediately below is another, in which the difficulties of the English tongue are bravely encountered (if not overcome) by some native, who prided himself, no doubt, on his profound acquaintance with that language. It certainly deserves a place amongst the "curiosities of literature." I copied it verbatim, and it runs as follows :—

"This bell is made by Koo-na-linn-guh-yah the priest * * * * and the weight 600 viss. No one body design to destroy this bell. Maulmain, March 30, 1855. He who destroyed to this bell, they must be in the great heell (hell) and unable to coming out."

The Palmyra palm is a tree almost invariably seen in proximity with religious buildings, and a sphinx-like animal in a sitting posture at the bottom of the steps is a figure of very frequent occurrence. Two, one on either side, generally guard the entrance to a temple; and four, one at each corner, are commonly seen at the base of a pagoda. The eyes, which are large and prominent, are often nothing more or less than the bottoms of green glass bottles, sent out to India, perhaps, by Bass or Allsopp, though these gentlemen can have little idea of the high position which the more durable part of their shipment occasionally attains. These sphinxes, which are sometimes truly gigantic, and might represent some extinct animal of a geological epoch long past, are constructed, like the pagodas, of plastered bricks.

There are in Burmah, as the reader may already have inferred, two distinct classes of religious edifices: the pagoda, already described as a solid mass of masonry erected to the memory of a Boodh, and generally supposed to contain sacred relics; and the temple, or image-house, which is used as a place of worship, and contains images of Gau-da-ma of different sizes and various substances, the most common being wood covered with gold-leaf, alabaster or marble, plaster, and metal. The illustration facing this is from a sketch I made of the exterior of one of these temples in Malay Street, Maulmain, and it is a good type of this class of building.

The several stages or roofs are indicative of a religious house, public building, or the dwelling of a person of rank. In the present instance there are five roofs, each one smaller than the one below; and thus they graduate towards the tee which surmounts the whole. Small pagodas may be noticed on either side. On the extreme right is a kyoung, monastery, or priest's house. The bell is seen suspended in front of the temple, and when an offering has been made, or some religious duty performed, it is generally struck by the devotee once or twice with a deer's horn; several of which are usually placed near the bell.

The next drawing is the interior of the same temple. The priests, who lived close by, made no objection to my going in alone, and remaining as long as I desired for the accomplishment of my task; and, though pretending indifference, I always found these worthy men very desirous of seeing how their favourite temple or pagoda looked on paper, and they were generally delighted and highly amused with the result. These temples are places of worship in a limited sense. There is no regular service; but on the days of the new and full moon, and on some other occasions, the men assemble in these edifices, present their offerings, and make their *shék-ho*, or homage, to the principal image. They also repeat prayers, using the rosary, whilst others are smoking and talking very much at their ease. The women may sometimes be seen in the further corner of the temple; but they generally remain outside, and occupy the adjacent bungalows, or open sheds, in which they pray, smoke, and talk by turns. The priests or monks (as the fraternity may be more correctly termed) do not interfere or in any way assist at the devotions of the people.

To return, however, to our sketch, which is highly characteristic of the interior of a Burman temple. In the centre is a gigantic image of Gau-da-ma, occupying the whole of the space from the ceiling to the altar. It is surrounded by images in a standing posture, some of them of gigantic proportions, and all are thickly covered with gold-leaf, with the exception of the head and part of the neck of each idol, which are white. As will be seen by the sketch, they are right jolly-looking gods, and as such are typical of the people and their religion. The latter, indeed, appears to be wholly divorced from everything like solemnity. In fact the Burman makes his god even such an one as himself—a laughter-loving, jovial being, much given to amusement and social intercourse. And as he connects very little solemnity with his religion, so he appears devoid of any feeling of sanctity as regards his temples and religious edifices. Fanaticism, too, would appear to find no place in his belief. His temples may be freely

Exterior of a Burman Temple, Malay Street, Maulmain.

entered, and his objects of worship examined by the stranger in race and infidel in creed, without calling forth any evidence of dislike or outraged religious feeling. Nevertheless their religion has, it is easy to perceive, a strong hold on their imagination, and is interwoven, in a remarkable manner, with their whole life from the cradle to the grave. Their grand religious festivals, on which occasions they postpone business and repair by thousands to their favourite pagodas and temples, to present offerings and repeat prayers to their gods, are all so many holidays and seasons of amusement and social intercourse. Added to this, it must be remembered that the priests, though a distinct class, are essentially one with the people; and there are few families who have not same male relation who is a member of a neighbouring Kyoung.

In the act of worshipping, the hands are joined and held to the forehead, and a flower or flowers, intended as an offering, are sometimes clasped in them. Umbrellas are also brought as offerings. These are often very pretty and made with much taste. The material employed is chiefly paper, generally white ornamented with gilt, and occasionally other colours are employed. They are also decorated with gilt pendants, and the long stems are not unlike barbers' poles. Bunches of flowers, flower-pots with plants, and little flags, are also common offerings. On a long board fronting the altar saucers of brown ware are usually placed, containing cocoa-nut oil and wicks which are burnt before the idol. Yellow cloth is very frequently wrapped round the images, and supplies the place of gold-leaf; it is likewise used for the robes of the priests, being the sacerdotal colour.

Maulmain is a pretty specimen of an eastern town. The streets are for the most part shaded with trees, amongst which the glossy jack is conspicuous. Wells are of frequent occurrence, at which Burman maidens may be seen bathing and drawing water at all hours of the day. At intervals, wooden structures on wheels, and sometimes constructed of solid materials, are placed at the road side, containing vessels of drinking-water for the benefit of the wayfarer, and this commendable custom is observed in all Burman towns. The main street runs parallel with the river. On either side are Burman houses and bazaars. Close to the main wharf is a large *puckah* building, comprising the offices of the deputy-commissioner, treasury, master-attendant's office, office of the collector of customs, and marine storekeeper. *Gharries*, the vehicles in general use in Maulmain, Rangoon, and other parts of India, and which answer to the European cabs, are frequently observed waiting for hire in the streets.

There are other good *puckah* buildings occupied chiefly by the offices of various mercantile firms and shopkeepers. The artillery barracks are of brick. The European and native infantry barracks are in the neighbourhood of the great pagoda, and near these is situated St. Matthew's episcopal church, a pretty building (constructed, however, of wood) capable of containing eight hundred people. It is lofty and cool, and like all churches in India is hung with *punkhas*. The post-office, police, assistant commissioners', and Tseekay's courts occupy a range of wooden buildings, and near this is the library and government school-house. The stranger should also pay a visit to the premises of the American Baptist Mission, including a chapel and printing establishment; here he will see the mission press in full activity, and worked by natives. From this press has issued the whole Bible in Burman language, dictionaries, and many tracts and elementary school-books, as well as various publications in the Taleing and Karen dialects. The American Baptist Mission was founded by Dr. Judson at Rangoon in 1812, since which Christian communities have been founded amongst the Burmans at Rangoon, Ava, Akyab, Sandoway, Maulmain, Tavoy, and Mergui; but the white teachers have found more disciples amongst the Karens and other tribes inhabiting Burmah than amongst the Burmans proper.

(See Chapter XXI.) In the neighbourhood of Maulmain and Tavoy are many low-lying paddy fields which are cultivated regularly, but a great deal of ground lies waste, being occupied by jungle and grass common. This arises in a great measure from the extreme scantiness of the population, though the people have greatly increased since the occupation of the provinces by the British. The total number of inhabitants was then estimated at 90,000. The following is the result of the census of 1855-56:—

	Amherst, exclusive of Maulmain.	Tavoy.	Mergui.
European and other Christian inhabitants	28	61	195
Talaings and Burmese	51,206	46,112	18,590
Shans and Thoungthoos	6,926	139	2,668
Karens	22,492	4,775	5,403
Chinese	539	1,024	955
Malays	1,592	76	1,340
Natives of India	4	680	1,699
	82,787	52,867	30,850

To this must be added the population of Maulmain, which in the same census is given as follows :—

Number of Men	18,021
„ Women	11,610
„ Children	14,052
	43,683
Add to this the foregoing, viz. Amherst	82,787
Tavoy	52,867 *
Mergui	30,850
The grand total will be	210,187

Which may be taken at least as an approximation to the truth. The population is steadily on the increase.

A great number of the houses of Maulmain are now tiled; but this improvement is being effected by a somewhat arbitrary enactment, which interdicts the use of thatch to a whole district at once, under severe penalties, which, in the case of native houses, is tantamount to pulling them down, for the

* According to the census of April, 1857, the population of Tavoy is 54,074.

frail erections are not often capable of supporting a roof of either tiles or shingles; and besides, these rise to such an exorbitant price in consequence of the extraordinary demand for them, that they are quite beyond the means of the greater number of Burmans. On returning to Maulmain towards the end of the wet season, I was astonished to find a large district of the town nearly roofless, and as the rain still came down in heavy showers the inhabitants were in a miserable plight. Some had entirely forsaken their now useless houses, and many deaths amongst the sick and aged were reported in consequence of this unusual exposure to the weather. The commissioner, Colonel Sir Archibald Bogle, now absent in Europe, was, I believe, the originator of this ingenious plan for depopulating the town.

The dingie-wallahs or boatmen, the dhobees or washermen, and the domestic servants are all foreigners; the latter are generally Madrassees.

CHAPTER V.

Administration of the Tenasserim Provinces—The Officers to whom it is entrusted—Scenery in the Neighbourhood of Maulmain—Damathat—Yearly Visit of the Shans to Maulmain—Their Ponies and Boxes.

MAULMAIN is the seat of government of the Tenasserim provinces. The officers who administer civil justice are divided into four classes, viz.—

1. The Commissioner.
2. The assistants to ditto.
3. The Tseekais.
4. Goung Gyouks.

The commissioner is, *de facto*, the governor of the Martaban and Tenasserim provinces under the supreme government of India. He sits in session at least once a month to try criminal cases; he also holds a court daily for receiving petitions from the inhabitants, and civil appeals from the decisions of the assistants to the commissioner. These likewise try cases, but with a limitation; and appeals may be made from their courts to that of the commissioner's. The tseekay's court is a small-cause court. He is subordinate to the deputy-commissioner, to whom appeals are made from his decisions. Besides the officers above enumerated, there are three other classes appointed to administer police duties, viz.—

5. Goungs.
6. Thoogyees.
7. Peons.

A peon is subordinate to goungs in towns, and to thoogyees in villages. His duties are those of a constable. A goung is subordinate to the tseekay of his town; and a thoogyee is subordinate to the goung gyouk of his division. The duty of a goung and of a thoogyee is to inquire into all offences occurring within his jurisdiction, and to bring all suspected persons before their immediate superior. A tseekay in a town and a goung gyouk in village districts are respectively subordinate to the assistant-commissioner of the jurisdiction. It is the duty of a tseekay and goung gyouk to take cognizance of all offences within their jurisdiction, to superintend their subordinates, to convey to their superior all persons apprehended by themselves or those under them, and to cause the attendance of prosecutors and witnesses when a case is tried. The police of Maulmain are under the immediate control of the magistrate. The town is divided into five districts, each of which is under a goung, or native head of police. These goungs are responsible each for his own district to the magistrate, to whom they report daily.

The decisions of the courts are, I believe, generally characterised by a spirit of fairness; and it can hardly be doubted by an unbiassed observer that the rule of the Company, in this part of India at least, is just and merciful, and confers an immense boon on the people, who, when governed by the Burman king, were all slaves; both life and property being at the mercy of a capricious tyrant, under whose sway population actually decreased. In British Burmah all have equal rights, and all are under the protection of the law; and, though a commissioner may sometimes play a few arbitrary pranks, yet he cannot chop off heads and seize property as he lists; every man dwells safely under his own vine and fig-tree, which, being interpreted, means his own jack and his own plaintain tree.

The neighbourhood of Maulmain is extremely beautiful. In the month of November, after the rains were over and the north-east monsoon had set in, I visited Damathat—a romantic spot about twenty miles from Maulmain, on the river Gyne. Here, as in every other part of Burmah, the highest hills are crowned with pagodas, adding much to the picturesqueness of the scenery. Going up the country in one of their row-boats is by no means disagreeable; they are extremely comfortable, and about a third of the space is covered with a kind of thatched tilt. Under this is a flat boarded floor, on which you place a mattress and pillow. With a good companion, books, and a sufficient stock of provisions, this mode of locomotion is pleasant enough. At Damathat we explored a large temple-cave, in which were shrines for the devout Boodhist, and images of Gau-da-ma innumerable.

This is the season at which the Shans (a tribe of Siamese from the north of Burmah) visit Maulmain in considerable numbers, bringing with them for sale ponies and round lacquered boxes. The former were this year much enhanced in price, in consequence of a considerable number being purchased by government. I saw a very good pony, but one which a few years ago would not have fetched more than eighty or one hundred rupees, sold for two hundred and fifty. Buying the animals, as the purchaser must, without any further knowledge of them than what he can obtain by a cursory inspection, is attended with some risk; but he has at least this advantage, that he generally sees them at their worst—

rough from the jungles, and tired with a long journey. If sound, they improve vastly with rest, food, and good grooming. The lacquered boxes vary in price according to the size, and are both pretty and useful. The Burmans use them as betel boxes.

CHAPTER VI.

Difficulty of communication between Maulmain and the Southern Provinces of British Burmah—The Moscos—The Reef called "The Cows"—Scenery of the Tavoy River—Town of Tavoy—The Quay and Pier—Sketch of the principal Zayat—Burman Life and Manners at Tavoy.

THE communication between Maulmain and the southern stations, both for mails and passengers, is very uncertain; more so, perhaps, than in any other part of India. The whole of Hindostan might be in the hands of the rebels, and all the Europeans in India have been massacred in a manner most unique and amusing to such fiendish savages as lately practised their diabolical cruelty in various parts of the country, yet months would possibly elapse before the benighted inhabitants of Tavoy and Mergui could gain the slightest inkling of what had taken place, and at last they would probably learn it by some vessel being wrecked on the coast, when perchance an English newspaper, containing "the latest intelligence viâ Marseilles," might be washed ashore; or the fact would perhaps be announced by an invasion of the territory by the King of Burmah. An inhabitant of the Great Cocoa, or the Little Andaman, would often gain a better idea of what was going on in the world than a British resident in the remoter settlements of the Tenasserim provinces. The communication is nominally kept up once a month by the Hon. Company's steamer "Pluto;" that is to say, when she happens to be stationed at Maulmain. When I first arrived in Burmah this vessel was undergoing repairs at Calcutta, and, as the south-west monsoon had set in, communication with the southern stations by means of native boats was out of the question. The only way of despatching a mail under these circumstances is by native runners overland. The Pluto returned to Maulmain about the middle of June, and by the courtesy of her commander, Captain Baker, I was at last enabled to reach Tavoy, where a day or two previously the terrible news of the revolt of the Bengal army had arrived by a chance vessel. A short but decided break in the weather enabled us to make a safe and agreeable passage and to obtain a fine view of the Tenasserim coast, which is kept in sight the whole distance. The next day we passed the Moscos, pretty densely-wooded islets, which, rising abruptly from the surface of the blue water, tower to the sky and seem to rest on nought but their own dark shadows. They are the resort of the sea-swallow. It hangs on the rocks its curious angular nest, so famous for its edible properties, and which at Maulmain is worth its weight in silver. These islets are in three groups, viz., the northern, the middle, and the southern Moscos. The Chinese possess a monopoly of these nests, which they purchase annually from government.

To reach the Tavoy river a vessel from the

northward has to run several miles south of the town of that name in order to double a neck of land which separates the river from the sea. Near the mouth is a dangerous reef called "the Cows," "formed," says Mason, "of porphyritic granite containing large crystals of flesh-coloured felspar. It is probably so called from its resemblance to the colour of a red cow; but tradition says that these rocks were originally a drove of cows which opposed Boodhism, and attempted to cross the river to beat down the pagoda opposite on Tavoy point; but, the divinity looking out from the pagoda, exclaimed, 'Those are not cows but rocks;' when they were all immediately changed to stone." The scenery of the river is beautiful and romantic in the extreme. Here are low-lying paddy fields on which enormous slate-coloured buffaloes, with retreating horns of great length, are lazily grazing, and there are towering hills magnificently wooded. A run of about thirty-four miles up the stream brings us to the little town of Tavoy, situated on the left bank of the river, in N. lat. 14° 4′, E. long. 98° 5′, and at a distance of about two hundred and twenty miles from Maulmain. It lies low, and is surrounded on three sides by paddy fields and on the fourth by the river. The houses are almost concealed from the view of a spectator on the river by the umbrageous trees—palms, plantains, jacks, cassias, and a hundred flowering shrubs that grow luxuriously around them.

The accompanying drawing is a view of the covered pier and the quay at Tavoy, taken from a building overlooking both. At the quay the market-boats are loading their fruits and wares for the bazaar. The next is a drawing I took of the principal *zayat* at Tavoy, which is a very characteristic building.

In every Burman town and village there is always one zayat, and in some towns more than one; they are frequently only open sheds, formed of bamboo and thatch. The zayat is a traveller's house or caravansary, and is always at the service of the people.

Quay and Pier, Tavoy.

There is no attendant; but the traveller or stranger spreads his bed, eats his food, and rests as long as he desires. The ground-floor of the one at Tavoy is much used by the vendors of fruit and different eatables. In this little town Burman life and manners are seen in all their simplicity; and the observer cannot but be struck by the frugality, contentment, happiness, and enjoyment of life manifested by the people. All appear well off, and have silks and gold ornaments at their command. None are very rich and none are very poor. The painful contrast of wealth, luxury, and gorgeous display with squalid poverty, suffering, and want, so often exhibited in more highly-civilized countries, is here unknown. All have enough and are contented with that sufficiency. The Burman eats his rice and ngapee, his staple food, chews his betel-nut, smokes his cigar, constructs his simple dwelling, and acts most fully on the divine aphorism that "sufficient for the day is the evil thereof." In the evenings the young men, who are athletic and well made, assemble in the streets and play at football, at which they are very expert; indeed, I have often witnessed scenes that have reminded me forcibly of lines in Goldsmith's Deserted Village.

The Burman houses are all constructed of the same materials and on the same plan. They are invariably raised from the ground, made of bamboo fastened with rattan, and thatched with the leaf of the water-palm, which grows in great abundance in this neighbourhood. The leaves are strung on a strip of split bamboo, and are then fit for use. Near most of the houses, supported by trellis-work, may be seen growing the piper-betel or betel-vine, the leaf of which is used for chewing with the nut of the areca or betel-palm. A piece of the latter is wrapped up in a leaf of the piper-betel, which is first smeared over with lime; the whole is then placed in the mouth, which it soon fills with a blood-red fluid. A Burman considers this as necessary as his daily food, and I have seen Europeans who are rather partial to it.

Under a great many houses a loom may be observed, at which a female is generally busy at work.

Many of the shops are mere sheds or stalls formed of bamboo and thatch. The vendors sit squatted down on the raised floor in the midst of their wares. Sometimes a fire is kindled on a few stones, and on this fritters, usually of rice, are fried.

CHAPTER VII.

The Burmans ethnologically considered—Costume of the Burmans—Tatooing—Ear-ornaments—Smoking.

The Burmans belong, ethnologically, to that group or variety of the human species characterised by a Mongolian physiognomy and a monosyllabic language. They have broad faces and high cheek-bones. Their dress is simple in the extreme on ordinary occasions, but at the same time not a little remarkable. The common dress of the men is the *In-gie* or *En-gie*, a white linen jacket; and a *Put-só*, or cotton cloth about four yards in length and one in breadth, which is put on round the hips, and when worn long extends to the ankles, but as it is frequently arranged it encircles only the middle. In the absence of the *in-gie* the long end of the *put-só* is generally thrown over one shoulder in a graceful manner, and then it not a little resembles a highland plaid and kilt. The men allow their black hair to grow long, and they fasten it in a knot at the top of the head. They seldom wear a moustache or any hair on the face. From the hips to the knees every male is most elaborately tatooed with a blue or black pigment, and their naked thighs remind one forcibly of the body of a serpent. This painful operation is done gradually and when very young. Boys are generally seen with a few figures on their thighs, which are extended by degrees until the whole process is accomplished. While being operated on they are drugged with opium to render their feelings less acute; and an overdose occasionally cuts the matter short by terminating the labours of the operator and the life of the patient at the same time. The upper part of the body is sometimes tatooed in patches, here and there, of a vermilion colour.

The usual costume of the female consists of an *in-gie* or white linen jacket, and the *te-miné*, while the *put-só* constitutes that of the male. The *te-miné* is a very scant garment quite innocent of crinoline. It is broad enough to wrap over a little way round the waist, where it is confined by one end being tucked under the other, and it extends to the feet. As it is neither tied, stitched, or fastened, except at the top as just described, it opens at every step taken by the wearer, exposing the greater part of one leg; but, as this is the universal custom, it is not considered immodest. A put-só or a te-miné made of silk is a costly article, but every Burman male and female possesses one or more which are worn on highdays and holidays. The women as well as the men wear their hair, which is black and glossy as the raven's wing, very long. The former comb it back from the forehead *à la Eugenie*, and fasten it in a knot at the back of the head. The young maidens adorn their dark locks with elegant flowers; which in England would be considered rare and beautiful exotics. Old women often wear only the "te-miné," and little children of both sexes go naked. Perhaps the most remarkable part of the female costume are the ear-ornaments in which they so much delight; and to introduce which an orifice of astonishing size is made in the lobe of the ear. The one most frequently worn is a cylinder of pinchbeck, enlarging at both ends, like a double trumpet. These ornaments are, however, made of different substances, and I have seen them formed of a solid roll of pure gold of great weight and value. In absence of any of them, a cigar, or some other article in constant use, is frequently thrust into the otherwise vacant orifice of the ear. For great occasions, the in-gie of the female is made of book-muslin, or some clear material, figured over or bespangled with gold. She wears no other covering on her head than that bestowed by nature. Smoking is universal amongst men, women, and children. Even infants at the breast are sometimes seen tugging hard at a cigar.

CHAPTER VIII.

Siam Hill—Early Walks in Burmah—Auriferous nature of the Soil—Loadstone Rock.

PURSUING the high road across the paddy fields about half-a-mile east from Tavoy, we reach a spot elevated fully one hundred feet above the town, and known as Siam Hill. Here is situated a large bungalow residence occupied by the deputy-commissioner. The site is very beautiful. The spacious compound, a park-like ground, is entered from the road through an avenue of the padouk—an ornamental evergreen tree of much beauty, the flower of which bears some resemblance to the laburnum, but is more showy and exceedingly fragrant. A thousand birds, of as many different colours, including the king-fisher, the bulbul, dove, crow-pheasant, mango-bird, paradise edolius, and others too numerous to mention, may be seen flying from tree to tree like living gems. On the right or west side a range of mountains running parallel with the river stretches away to the south, and in the rainy season here and there a water-fall may be seen gushing out from the thick foliage that clothes their sides. Next comes a splendid mass of tropical vegetation and trees of novel form, amongst which the palm tribe is conspicuous; then a carpet of the greenest grass is spread far and near, dotted over with herds of the small humped cattle of India. There, too, a band of priests may often be seen, clad from head to foot in robes of yellow, wending their way leisurely to some neighbouring kyoung or pagoda; each one pondering, no doubt, on the mysteries of Boodhism as he walks soberly along with bare feet and uncovered head, like a mendicant friar of Europe. A boy holds over him a Chinese umbrella to shield his shaven pate from the direct rays of a tropical sun. "On the south a silver stream, fringed with the dark foliage of wild fig-trees, and the thick straggling bushes of a species of hibiscus, covered with large yellow and red flowers, is seen pursuing its tortuous course beneath the shadows of Mount Burney, which rises twelve hundred feet above its southern bank. On the east 'hills peep o'er hills,' like the seats of a vast amphitheatre, bounded by Ox's Hump, rising in a most picturesque outline four thousand feet above the plains."

Even during the rains the European must not miss his early walk or ride, although he will most probably get drenched to the skin before his return; for the clouds having to discharge about two hundred inches of water in six months (sixty inches of which fell this year, 1857, in the single month of May), they cannot stand on ceremony, but pour down their contents in a most unmerciful patter, at all hours of the day and night. A greater drawback, perhaps, is the extreme sultriness of the morning, even before the sun has risen far above the horizon.

There are many pleasant rambles around

Tavoy; and, if the stranger takes his sketch-book, he will find an extensive field for the exercise of his art amongst the numerous monuments and edifices of this singular people. As he pursues his way many sounds strike on his ear, which to the lover of nature are agreeable in the extreme. The cawing of the ubiquitous crow, the cooing of the turtle-dove in the lone wood, the tinkle of the wooden bell attached to the neck of the huge buffalo, which may be seen cooling his hide in the soft mud of the paddy fields—all give a charm to these country solitudes. The gilded spires of a thousand towering pagodas* flash in the first rays of the rising sun, and the soft music of the little bells that are hung around the top is wafted on the breeze. Fruit-women, aged crones, and budding maidens, with baskets on their heads, and with stick in hand to keep off the crows, are wending their way to the township; while huge elephants stalk along the road in

* In Tavoy and the neighbourhood there are said to be one thousand monuments to Gau-dă-ma.

the same direction. Many beautiful trees, flowers, mosses, and ferns occur at every step; indeed, a flora, as novel to the European botanist as it is interesting and worthy of study, is spread out before him.

> The palm-tree waveth high,
> And fair the betel springs;
> And to the Indian maid
> The bulbul sweetly sings.

The geologist, too, will find an interesting field of inquiry. A great deal of quartz is seen in many directions; and the ground reminded me forcibly of the gold-fields of Australia. Indeed, there are strong indications of the auriferous nature of the soil. A well for the new jail on Siam Hill had been sunk about forty feet in the alluvial soil, without reaching the bottom; but on some of this soil being washed, under the direction of the officiating deputy-commissioner of Tavoy, Captain J. C. Haughton, who is himself an excellent practical geologist, a speck of the precious metal was discovered. I think it probable, both from the "prospect," or indication, and the nature of the country, that if in the dry season a sufficient number of shafts to test the ground were carried down, a remunerative gold-field would be discovered.

In company with the deputy-commissioner I paid a visit to a remarkable hill, upwards of a hundred feet high, situated about three miles north-west of Tavoy, on the summit of which is a large loadstone rock. The part that is buried in the soil is more highly magnetic than that exposed to the action of the air. We employed a man to quarry out a few fragments, which were strong enough to attract a small key considerably out of the perpendicular when suspended by a thread; and needles were easily rendered magnetic by being rubbed with a piece of the loadstone.

CHAPTER IX.

Burman Road-side Watering-places and Flagstaffs.

On the road-side, about three-quarters of a mile east of Tavoy, is one of those useful and characteristic erections for the benefit of the way-farer, where he may obtain a plentiful supply of the purest water, contained in earthen vessels placed in two niches made for that purpose. Near it is a Burman flagstaff, surmounted as usual by a tee, which is richly gilded. About a third of the way from the top is a wooden figure designed to represent the domestic cock, the national emblem of the Burmans or of Burmah. A very elaborate building of this kind is situated in the vicinity of the town. In that the entwined serpents are green and gold; the ground is a shining white, the top is richly gilt, and the whole forms a beautiful object as it flashes and glitters in a tropical sun. These edifices have a religious significance. Near the watering-place is a temple, the entrance to which is guarded by two enormous animals of the usual form, with glass-bottle eyes.

The peacock, so often found attached to these buildings, has evidently some religious bearing. No less than three are to be seen on the outside of the image-house just alluded to, as well as a remarkable animal only to be met with in Boodhist zoology.

One day as I was wandering near a kyoung on a Burman holiday, the priest, taking me by the hand, led me within and placed me by his side while he preached to a congregation of women, each one kneeling, with joined and uplifted hands, during the whole of his discourse, the pon-gyee holding a fan before his face the while. The Burmans are evidently a people of strong religious feeling, and it is a pity it should be so misdirected. They are also polite and kind to strangers, as was instanced on one occasion in particular, when during my morning walk I came upon a large party assembled in a spacious zayat, where they were celebrating some religious festival. They offered me cigars and refreshments, and finally a seat on the bungalow. Fruits, sweetmeats, and eatables of various descriptions, cups, saucers, and a great array of crockery, fine dresses, silks, gold ornaments, and musical instruments were to be seen *ad infinitum.*

A pagoda and a temple, in close proximity, when seen at a little distance crowning a hill-top, bear a great resemblance to a church and steeple; but the Christian philanthropist indulging himself in this pleasing delusion, would be greatly disappointed, on entering the supposed church, to find it full of uncouth idols and scattered over with the rubbish of former offerings.

The kyoung or priest's house is a kind of monastery, and is the national school of Burmah. In them, and in sheds adjoining, boys are daily instructed in reading, writing, and the elements of arithmetic. They squat down on the raised floor and write their

Burman Zayat, or Caravansary, Tavoy.

copies on black boards, using a piece of French chalk as a pencil. The more advanced pupils, however, may be seen writing, or rather engraving, on prepared strips of palm-leaf,* with an iron instrument pointed at both ends. Some of them exhibit great neatness of execution. They also show occasionally considerable skill in mathematical investigations, for the Deputy-Commissioner of Tavoy province assured me that he had seen the time of an eclipse calculated to within half an hour of the actual event at one of these schools.

The priests or monks superintend the studies of these boys, who are very regular in their attendance during the rainy season. The education thus received is entirely gratuitous, but the priests subsist by the voluntary contributions of the people.

* These strips of palm-leaf are about 20 inches long by $2\frac{1}{4}$ broad. A number of these, with a board of the same size on either side, form a book.

CHAPTER X.

Religious Festivals of the Burmans—Barges with Native Bands and Dancing Girls—Contrast between the Appearance and Costume of the Burmans on Ordinary and Extraordinary Occasions—A Burman Crowd—Devotions of the People at the Pagodas and Temples—An aged Woman worshipping.

In October (1857) I attended, for the sake of studying the manners and customs of the Burmans, several of their grand religious festivals, of which I shall now endeavour to give the reader some account.

On the 7th of October one of these fêtes took place at Shen-da-way or Old Tavoy, which place lies some few miles from the modern town, higher up the river. Thither, as to a place of pilgrimage, all the Burman world was flocking, and accompanied by a friend I repaired to the shrine to see how they manage these things in Burmah. We embarked with the tseekay, in the Deputy-

Commissioner's boat, which was taken in tow by two canoes full of active rowers, who made her bound over the water like a thing of life. The picturesque Tavoy river looked most beautiful as it wended its serpentine course through a country which for natural scenery is seldom equalled and still more rarely surpassed. One side is bordered for a considerable distance by the feathery frondage of the water-palm, which looks very much like the cocoa-nut palm without its trunk—as if the fronds had been cut off and stuck into the ground. On the other side the vivid green of the low paddy fields and slopes of the greenest sward were backed by high blue-looking hills of considerable elevation. The river was gay with long-prowed ornamented racing canoes full of brawny rowers, who seemed to throw the exuberance of animal strength and spirits into the enjoyment of the day.

But the most conspicuous and attractive objects were the barges in which were bands of music and dancing-girls. These barges are formed by two canoes lashed together, on which is placed a floor of planks, and on this a frame of bamboo is raised, open at the sides, and supporting a roof thatched with the leaves of the water-palm; a most effectual protection from the fierce and penetrating rays of a tropical sun. Each barge is towed by two canoes full of Burman rowers. The stern, from which streams the British ensign, is occupied by the band, the instruments composing which are unique, and objects of much curiosity to the European eye. There is a circular frame, in the interior of which small drums, or tom-toms, are placed, and the performer sits in the centre. Another circular frame contains round metallic plates which are beaten with a stick by a musician, who likewise occupies the centre. Cymbals, pieces of split bamboo, which are beaten one against the other, and a sort of flageolet, make up the Burman band. At the other end is a more interesting sight. Burman girls, in the most elaborate and costly dresses, are dancing to the somewhat discordant sounds of the instruments already described. On this occasion, however, they were not hired and professional dancers; but ordinary Burman damsels, and some were married women. Nothing, perhaps, strikes the stranger so much as the contrast between what appear to him the more than half-naked savages he takes this people to be when he first sees them in their every-day dress, in their rude houses and straggling villages, and the refinement, elaborate toilette, costly ornaments of gold, silks, and other paraphernalia they display on grand occasions. The quantity of highly-worked gold necklaces and pendants, chains, bangles or bracelets, ear-ornaments, rings, and precious stones, worn by these damsels, would astonish, and perhaps excite the envy of, many a European belle. The principal garment, the te-mine, is made of silk, striped in horizontal zigzag lines, in which red and yellow are the predominating colours. The in-gie is of lace, or embroidered book-muslin, and over the left shoulder is thrown a scarf of figured silk or gauze. The dancing is confined to the females, and is more a posturing than the exercise we understand by the term; the arms, hands, and fingers perform an important part, being turned and contorted in a most extraordinary manner. All the while an imperturbable gravity is preserved. The head is without any other covering than the thick black hair this people invariably possess. It is combed back from the forehead, fastened in a knot behind, and ornamented with flowers. They likewise rub sandal-wood powder and other cosmetics over their faces, so that the women often appear much fairer than they really are. As soon as one set of dancers is tired another starts up, and so on in constant succession. The whole performance is very monotonous, but appears to keep up an unflagging interest in the spectators, who are squatted around smoking cigars, chewing betel-nut, and in the seventh heaven of felicity and enjoyment.

From the landing-place a broad raised path led away through fields of waving paddy to pagoda-crowned hills and grassy slopes, across which the people were flitting in their gayest attire—all in the highest spirits, with countenances on which good humour, content, and kind feeling were evidently stamped. A Burman crowd, indeed, as far as my experience goes, is always well-behaved. There is no coarseness, rudeness, quarrelling, or drunkenness, and cynical must be that man's spirit who can look on in total apathy at so much innocent enjoyment and happy social intercourse as is manifested on such occasions, although he may lament that it should be in anyway connected with an idolatrous worship and an erroneous belief. Arrived at the pagodas and temples, the people suddenly turn from pleasure to devotion. Men, bearing ornamental paper umbrellas, fruits, flowers, and other offerings, crowd into the image-houses, present their gifts to the favourite idol, make their *shék-ho*, and say their prayers with all despatch. Others are gluing more gold-leaf on the face of the image, or saluting him with crackers, the explosion of which in no wise interferes with the serenity of the worshippers. The women for the most part remain outside, kneeling on the sward, just at the entrance of the temple, where a view can be obtained of the image within. On our way back, as the barges arrived at their respective villages, the landing-places were thronged with people to witness the return of their friends.

In a few days there was another pilgrimage down the river to Shoay-mowk-tee, where there was a shrine of great reputed sanctity. We were on the wharf by six o'clock A.M. just as the rising sun was flashing its first rays on the silver stream; which silently threaded its tortuous course through fields of paddy, backed by dark-looming mountains, half shrouded in wreaths of white vapour. Boats and barges, here and there, dotted the broad river, and every thing was much the same as on the former occasion, though I thought a little less life and gaiety was displayed; as if the actors, in this long comedy, were growing somewhat weary. Arrived at the landing-place we saw men, women, and children, up to their knees in mud, scrambling to the top of a steep bank, through the soft slime and yielding clay of the river; and we were fain to mount on the shoulders of two stout Burmans.

The principal temple being under repair, was much crowded by bamboo-scaffolding, and new pillars were being put up, each bearing an inscription with the name of the donor, who, no doubt considered himself much nearer Nieban by virtue of so meritorious an act. The umbrellas brought as offerings were so numerous that one could with difficulty thread a passage through them. Some were pure white, others white and gold, while many boasted all the colours of the rainbow. They were made of paper, beautifully cut into various patterns. There were numerous altars and images, and numberless little Gau-da-mas; but a deep niche or cave, at the far end of which was a fat idol with a yellow cloth wrapped round him, seemed a place of peculiar sanctity. This recess would have been quite dark had it not been for the numberless tapers of yellow wax that were burning before the image. The closeness of the place, the smoke from the candles, and the fumes from the quantity of crackers constantly being let off, rendered respiration almost impossible. An old pon-gyee however, the only one I ever saw in a temple, seemed quite in his element; his shaven bristly head and coarse features looking ugly enough to serve for some favourite idol; and he seemed a fitting embodiment of so senseless and degrading a worship. Offerings of flowers, paper ornaments, flags, and candles were scattered about in profusion. The beating a bell with a deer's horn, the explosion of crackers, and the rapid muttering of prayers, made up a din of sounds, the suitable accompaniment of so misdirected a devotion. The worshippers have little idea of reverence during their prayers; for, though their attitude is certainly one of deep humility (the same, however, they observe in the presence of their great men), yet the mind is evidently little impressed. A brief form of words is gabbled over, beads are counted, a meritorious work is performed, and a certain amount of merit is supposed to be earned; but the heart is unmoved, the moral feelings are unawakened. There are of course some exceptions to this general rule. I remember in particular, on this occasion, observing a very aged woman who appeared to be deeply absorbed. It was an affecting sight to behold the silver head and withered form bowed low in humility, whilst the feeble shrivelled hands were raised in mute but earnest supplication to the dumb idol, in which she had been taught to see a present God; and acting up, as she was, to the best of her belief and knowledge, I could not but hope and believe that she was viewed with pity and acceptance by her Omniscient Creator.

CHAPTER XI.

Buffalo Fights—Boat-racing—Rites of Cremation—Burman Pooay.

TAVOY is remarkable for its grand annual buffalo fight. This exciting but barbarous diversion is here celebrated with all its ancient pomp and circumstance. At Mergui and Martaban it is also carried on to some extent. The tseekay presides on these occasions and acts as umpire. This diversion, which appears to retain a strong hold on the affections of the Tavoyers, takes place on a large plain close to the town, at the time of the full moon in October, and towards the close of the rains, which for months have saturated the ground with a deluge of water. For many weeks previous to the actual commencement of the sport, preparations are going on in which the liveliest interest is manifested by all classes of the people. In several parts of the town enormous buffaloes may be seen, destined to take a part in the approaching contest. They are owned by different districts and townships; and each one is an object of attraction and interest to those who have chosen it for their champion. They sit around the huge animal for hours smoking, chatting, and arguing on its capabilities and disposition. They cut for it the freshest grass, and lead it by a cord passed through its nose to the soft mud in which it delights to wallow, and to the cooling stream, where it may often be seen nearly immersed, its broad black nose only raised above the water. At last the long-looked-for day arrives. On the spot before mentioned a number of sheds made of bamboo and thatch, the floors of which are raised several feet from the ground, are erected. All these are crammed with spectators, and thousands more occupy the inclosed space. At length a movement in a certain direction is perceived, cymbals and drums announce the arrival of the first buffalo, which forthwith makes its appearance in great state. First of all come a crowd of nearly naked men dancing, shouting, and cutting the most grotesque antics. Next walks the buffalo under a canopy, and surrounded by a white cord held out by some of its supporters. A man leads it by a cord passed through its nose, and it is thus paraded round the ground. In a little while another movement is visible, and the excitement becomes more intense. Another buffalo is seen in the distance slowly wending its way to the scene of conflict. He soon arrives on the field, and is led towards his antagonist. The flags which have been held before the eyes of either animal are now removed, and each is mounted by a Burman, who retains his seat on the animal's back as long as possible, at the imminent risk of being precipitated on the horns, or trampled under the feet, of the contending and enraged buffaloes. No sooner do the animals catch sight of each other than they rush furiously to the combat, and the clash of their massive foreheads may be heard at some distance. And now the excitement of the people is at its height; the mass of human beings sways to and fro and closes around the buffaloes. Peons with long bamboos beat back the crowd. Men interested in the victory of their champion buffalo urge him on in every possible manner. The fray seldom lasts longer than a few minutes, when one of the animals suddenly comes to the conclusion that discretion is the better part of valour, and remembering, no doubt, the maxim of Hudibras, rushes from the field through the midst of the spectators, whilst its antagonist follows at its heels. On they go amid the shouts and laughter of the people, who generally bring them to a stand at a greater or less distance from the original scene of conflict, when a more furious and lasting fight often ensues, in which the tables are sometimes turned, the fugitive becoming in its turn the conqueror. Various bets are made on the issue of the contest, and as soon as it is decided the victorious party re-appear on the ground, yelling, shouting, dancing, making the most frantic gestures, rolling in the mud—their dishevelled hair all the while streaming in the wind. Men, boys, and women join in a wild dance; and, lastly, the victorious buffalo is paraded around the ground by his partizans. He is decked out with flowers, caressed, and in one instance I observed a man kiss the huge brute on his forehead several times with great gusto. After a short interval another pair of buffaloes arrive on the field, when a similar scene takes place. In some cases one of the animals, being imbued, it would appear, with "peace-at-any-price" principles, altogether refuses the combat, and bolts from the ground, to the great disgust of its friends and patrons. The sport continues for two days, during which time eight pair of buffaloes are brought into the field; but the town continues in a state of excitement for some time, and the victorious buffaloes are paraded through the streets decked out in various ways, and accompanied by a number of the winning party, all dressed in holiday attire. The young men, clad only in silk *put-sos*, and gold chains about their necks, dance, whenever the procession stops, to the musical instruments by which it is accompanied.

At this season, also, the *Lhay peyine pooay*, or boat race, takes place, which is certainly a more agreeable sight than that of which I have just endeavoured to give the reader an idea. From a high building close to the water's side I was able to obtain a capital view of the whole scene, which was one of the gayest description. A dense mass of Burmans—men, women, and children—all dressed in their most brilliant silks, and glittering with ornaments, gold chains, necklaces, rings, and precious stones, occupied every available spot of ground; yet all were well-conducted, polite, and accommodating; and, if a European passed through them, a way was promptly opened for him, and every respect exhibited. The umpire's boat was fastened near the wooden pier that juts out into the river. The racing canoes are thirty or forty feet long, and very narrow. Their prows rise obliquely from the water to a considerable height, and they have a somewhat classical appearance. Down either side of each boat sit fifteen or sixteen athletic rowers, with paddles about three feet in length, which they use with great dexterity. One man stands at the prow, and another at the stern to steer. The former, if his boat wins, immediately throws himself into the most extraordinary and grotesque attitudes, shouting and gesticulating as only a Burman can; all this being intended as a demonstration of victory. On one occasion, the steersman of the winning boat overbalanced himself in his eagerness and fell into the water, in which a Burman is as much at home as on land; but the accident occasioned his canoe to lose the race. A great deal of betting goes on all the time, and considerable sums of money change hands.

Before leaving Tavoy I had an opportunity of witnessing the rites of cremation as practised by the Burmans, which, when the bodies of priests have to be disposed of, form the most extraordinary of their religious dramas. The gay and festive nature of the Burman religion, and the total absence of all solemnity in the performance of what we should have supposed the most serious and sacred offices of religion to which I have before alluded, are very fully demonstrated at a funeral, which appears to be regarded as an excellent practical joke, a season for the exhibition of buffoonery and mirth. On this occasion the bodies of two pon-gyees, which had been previously embalmed, were to be burnt with the usual amount of serio-comic display. As I approached the open space or plain in which this strange ceremony was to take place, I saw a grand ornamental cenotaph on wheels, in which the coffins were enclosed, slowly moving along amidst a concourse of people all dressed in their holiday attire. Two long ropes were attached to the car, and by means of these it was dragged forward by eager volunteers towards the spot where the burning was to take place—a space paved with stones and surrounded by low brick walls, in which an opening was left for the passage of the funeral carriage.

On arriving within a few yards of this enclosure a sort of sham contest was enacted, the two parties holding the ropes tugging and drawing in opposite directions, one set pulling one way and the other in an opposite direction, greatly to the amusement of the spectators, till at last one of them was supposed to be victorious, having succeeded in dragging the cenotaph in triumph to the enclosed space before alluded to. And now a number of women arrived, each bearing a basket filled with fruit and vegetables intended as offerings for the priests. I counted no less than seventy or eighty of these. Several pon-gyees were in attendance, and one of them superintended the division of the presents, which he accomplished at last apparently to his satisfaction, and squatting down with the other priests by the side of the car they repeated a few prayers; the people betaking themselves to the same attitude, and muttering some words in chorus. This over, a buffoon displayed his antics, and then a long rope was stretched from the car to a tree at some distance. A rocket was attached to this cord and subsequently fired for the purpose of igniting the combustibles around the bodies. This not having the desired effect, fire was applied to the cenotaph in several places, most of the ornaments and devices with which it was decorated having previously been removed to serve for another occasion.

The car was soon in a blaze, and after a short time the blistered remains of the bodies were exposed to view; but the pyre was kept burning till all was reduced to ashes. The bright azure of the sky, the vivid green of the grassy plain, and the brilliant colours displayed by the congregated people, combined to form a spectacle both gay and picturesque, but as unlike a funeral as it is possible to conceive. Such a scene carries one back in imagination to classic times, and brings to memory Homer's graphic description of the burning of Patroclus, although here there was no "sad sacrifice" of Trojan captives, nor even of the inferior animals, which, indeed, would be utterly opposed to the principles of Boodhism. A writer in the Maulmain Directory gives a graphic account of one of these spectacles in that town, and which I here transcribe. "In the instance," he says, "of the preparation for the funeral rites no means are spared to have, according to their notions, a magnificent display. The body of the priest is covered with gold leaf and laid in a richly-ornamented coffin. Wooden tubes of various lengths, from about six to ten feet, which, for the want of a more appropriate term, may be called *rockets*, strongly bound with rattans, and filled with the common ingredients of gunpowder, are fastened to the axles of low carriages of four wheels. Surmounting these are placed figures of men and animals of the most grotesque description, formed of light materials, some of them of enormous size, and in the formation of the whole the study and design of the devisers seem to be to deviate from nature rather than to imitate it.

"Every village or district has its body of young men and women formed into separate bands, and at the head of each band is a Burman chosen for the brilliance of his wit, or any other attribute he may possess, which entitles him generally to be acknowledged as the cock of the walk. The bands dress themselves up in uniforms, and by dint of practice, for a month or two before the ceremony takes place, acquire great skill in attitudinising and accompanying the different figures they execute with songs appropriate to the occasion, laudatory to themselves, and to the particular village to which each separate band belongs. When the time is near for the conclusion of the ceremony, they pass in procession through the town, and visit the houses of the Commissioner and of those Europeans who are agreeable to receive it, preceded by a party of richly-dressed women singing and dancing, and responded to by a larger company of men who follow, wearing some badge or dress to distinguish one band from the other. On they go, white elephants, giants, horses, rams, buffaloes, dragons, and the likenesses of nothing in heaven above or on the earth beneath innumerable. The songs composed for the occasion are highly in praise of themselves, their villages, and replete with good wishes for the authorities and others whom they visit. The processions last for several hours, when the whole move off to prepare for the next day.

"On the succeeding morning the streets of the town are filled with men, women, and children in their holiday dress, moving towards the Burmese burial-ground, situated at the back of the Maulmain hills, which is the spot selected for the final exhibition and the performance of the funeral rites. By nine o'clock most of the population of the town take up their position on the heights to the westward of it, from whence they could look down on the plain below; some on the plain, some on the sides of the hills, having the appearance at a distance of bees swarming round a hive. Tents formed of handkerchiefs, placed on bamboo sticks, temporary sheds covered with leaves, thousands of umbrellas, the varied and brilliant colours of the Burman dresses, with a white tent occupied by several ladies and gentlemen of the community, pitched in the centre of an animated and easily-pleased mass of people, with the sun shining on the glittering golden ornaments worn by the Burmese, form (assisted by the picturesque nature of the country) as pretty and gay a sight as any could wish to see. If we compute the number of spectators at these scenes at twelve thousand, we should not probably be far from the truth.

"The body of the priest is in a car of state, and placed under a shed decorated with spires, and situated at a distance of about four to five hundred feet. Each village has a wooden gun about fifteen feet in length, and diameter of bore about nine inches. This gun is stuffed to the muzzle with pyrotechnic materials, and is mounted on a car which runs on four wheels. On the top of the gun a figure is placed, sometimes the effigy of an archer, sometimes a crab, sometimes a beeloo, or any fanciful device, according to the taste of the villagers. These guns are now fired in rotation, being placed opposite the car in which the body of the pon-gyee lies, first of one village then of another, and so on, pouring vast clouds of smoke, hissing louder than a hundred steam-engines, and careering across the plain as chance—for they are not guided—conducts their rapid movements. When the material is all exhausted the machine gradually stops, and the men to whom it belongs rush up, dance, and sing around it. The great point to gain is to be so fortunate as to direct your gun so as to go straight a-head, and strike the car in which the body of the priest lies, and for the combustibles with which the car is crammed to be ignited from the fire of the gun, and the car with the body blown up. On such an event happening great is the joy of the chosen band, and great will be the luck for the ensuing year of the villages from whence the gun has been brought. During the many years we have been here we never recollect one to have hit their object; some deviate to the right and some to the left, while others break down and are thus 'stopped in mid career.' On one occasion the shed was struck by a rocket, and owing to a train of gunpowder being laid on the ground it ignited. The district owning the white elephant ayook (effigy) was the fortunate one of the day. Many doons (rockets) went near the car, and many more went off at an angle of the shed into the jungle. Shortly after the successful ayook had performed its duty the festival was brought to a close, by the few remaining rockets being sent off, and the car set on fire by order of the pon-gyees. We have, unfortunately, been witness to several deaths and severe injuries to persons from the rockets, which, after they are once ignited, are not in any way controlled; consequently the least inequality of the ground may turn the car (which runs on four wheels, and on which the rocket is fixed horizontally) off at any angle, and, before the lookers-on know where they are, the machine rushes down on them with the velocity of a steam-engine, overturning every obstacle, and only stopping when all the materials with which it is charged are burnt out.

"During the day the town presents quite a deserted appearance. The gharrie-wallahs reap a plentiful harvest, asking as much as from six to ten rupees, and refusing to let their gharries out unless remunerated at these exorbitant rates.

"This interesting and imposing ceremony, which had annually been performed in all its grandeur and magnificence, has in a great measure been discountenanced by the authorities, who either fear their power and capability of preserving the peace of the town during its continuance, or are repugnant to its being performed on the sabbath, a day which is, unfortunately, always chosen for its celebration."

The Burman delights in every species of

amusement, and is especially fond of a *pooay*, or play, of which there are a great number just at the close of the rainy season. A play is given by one individual at his own expense, and it is perfectly free to every one. A very curious display of this nature is a doll-pooay. A long stage is erected in a convenient spot, where a large space can be obtained in front for the spectators. As evening approaches, and some hours before the appointed time, the people take up their position here; bringing mats, cigars, and betel-nut, they squat down at their ease and determine to make a night of it. In due time a number of dressed-up figures, about the size of large dolls, are let down upon the stage; the action of these puppets is controlled by strings, which are managed by men hidden from view. They make these figures act their parts very cleverly, and cause them to hold dialogues with each other; the voices seeming to come from the dolls. Hundreds of Burmans, both men and women, sit patiently till morning watching the progress of the play with unflagging interest. A European, however, may very well satisfy his curiosity in an hour.

The Burmans are proverbially indolent, but the women are much more industrious than the men. The latter show much skill as carpenters and blacksmiths.

CHAPTER XII.

Climate—South-west Monsoon—Time of its commencement and the period of its duration—Average fall of Rain—Temperature during the Rains—Cool and Hot Seasons—Their respective average Temperatures.

SOON after I arrived at Maulmain the south-west monsoon set in with almost unusual violence. Much damage was done on the coast, and several ships were driven back by the violence of the wind. The rain at first came down in heavy showers, and it certainly was a great relief from the intense heat that immediately preceded it. After a few days it became a continued pour, saturating the air with moisture, which penetrated everything and everywhere in a remarkable manner. Under its influence books fall to pieces, clothes become mildewed and worthless, and a blue mould creeps over walls and furniture. The everlasting patter of the rain is only varied by the human-like voice of the small house-lizard or gecko, and the cry of the *touk-tay* (a large lizard also found in dwellings), which chimes in now and then like the striking of a cuckoo-clock, which the very extraordinary sound it makes much resembles.

To a stranger this season is particularly depressing, at least I judge so from my own experience; and Mrs. Judson says, not less truly than beautifully, when writing from Maulmain, during the absence of her husband at this time on a sea-voyage for the benefit of his failing health:—

The wild south-west monsoon has risen,
With broad grey wings of gloom,
While here from out my dreary prison
I look as from the tomb, alas!
My heart another tomb.

Upon the low-thatched roof the rain
With ceaseless patter falls;
My choicest treasures bear its stains,
Mould gathers on the walls—would Heaven
T'were only on the walls.

Sweet mother, I am here alone
In sorrow and in pain,
The sunshine from my heart has flown,
It feels the driving rain. Ah me,
The chill, and mould, and rain!

In this part of Burmah the south-west monsoon generally sets in about the 20th of May amidst storm and tempest, thunder and lightning, wind and rain, and in October it takes its departure in a like boisterous manner. During the five months that it prevails the rain often pours down for days together without cessation, and the sun is obscured for weeks. There are, however, occasional breaks in the weather, when the sun, for a short period, peeps through the dense canopy of clouds that so tempers his fierce rays at what would otherwise be a season of intense and almost unendurable heat. The average fall of rain for the last five years has been, Dr. Walter informed me, 194·28 in.; but, according to the tables kept by Dr. Morton from the commencement of the year 1841 to the end of the year 1846, the average fall of rain during that time was 216½ inches. The greatest amount of rain ever recorded as having fallen in one day was on the 27th of May, 1857, when 12·75 in. was registered, and within the week 40·27 in.

were measured by Dr. Walter, who used two separate gauges, and took every precaution to guard against error. At this time, and while the rains last, the temperature is remarkably uniform, the thermometer ranging between 76° and 82°. Towards the end of the wet season the rain falls in showers with a constantly increasing interval between them, and on its total cessation, when the north-east monsoon sets steadily in, the cool part of the year commences, and continues till the middle of February. The sun then regains its power, and the heat increases daily till the south-west monsoon again brings a deluge of waters.

This year (1857) rain fell at intervals during the early part of November. At the change of the monsoon, and during the gradual cessation of the rain, coughs, colds, and fevers are very prevalent. The mornings now become cool and pleasant, though often spoilt by a dense fog. A good gallop or a brisk walk at sun-rise is very enjoyable, and, after a bath and breakfast, the European feels less disposed than usual to quarrel with a tropical climate, and he is fain to confess that if it were equally good all the year round he would desire nothing better. The thermometer at this time of the year seldom reaches 90° in the shade, and occasionally falls as low as 56°. The prevailing wind is easterly. It is while the cool season prevails that the greatest thermometric range is observed, which is sometimes as great as 30° in one day. During the succeeding hot months the thermometer in the middle of the day is not often below 92° in the shade.

The town of Tavoy lies low and is nearly surrounded by paddy-fields and other prolific sources of malaria. The most common diseases are intermittent fevers and dysentery; but the climate is on the whole healthy, and, generally speaking, by no means inimical to the constitution of the European.

CHAPTER XIII.

The principal Exports — Teak Trees — Varieties — Number of Trees to be procured annually from the Forests—Rice—Its quality—The Time of Year to sow the Paddy—Rice Harvest—Agricultural Implements of the Burmans—Valuable Dyes.

THE Tenasserim provinces offer a fine field, and one comparatively little known, for commercial enterprise and British capital. The two principal exports are teak timber and rice; but to these might be added sugar, coffee, spices, indigo, opium, tobacco, cotton, and other valuable products.

A few straggling teak-trees are indigenous in the northern portion of Tavoy province: *i. e.*, further south than 15° 11′ north latitude; but 15° 20′ is generally reckoned as its southern limit. The best teak grows in considerable quantities on the rivers Ye, Wengo, Gyne, Thoung-yeen, and Attaran. The *kyoon-paroon* and *kyoon-kyouk*, or rock teak, are the two principal varieties. The former is a light-coloured open-grained wood, which floats almost as soon as it is felled. It attains to a large size, and reaches maturity in eighty years. The other species is a much harder, closer-grained wood, and of slower growth, not reaching its prime in less than 150 or 200 years. The enterprising merchants of Maulmain, seconded by native woodmen, have discovered and worked these teak forests, bringing the timber to town, and there preparing and shipping it to the home market. This wood was first exported direct to England from the Tenasserim provinces in 1839; and it is calculated that 2,100 full-sized trees, or about 3,000 tons, per annum, can be procured from the teak districts, without encroaching on those trees which have not yet arrived at maturity.

The export of rice from Maulmain has been for some years steadily on the increase, and it has been pronounced by a well-qualified judge to be equal to the best Carolina rice. The time for sowing the paddy is the latter end of May, or at the commencement of the south-west monsoon, and it soon springs up from the saturated ground. From December to January is the rice harvest. It is trodden out of the ear by buffaloes, which, indeed, are used for ploughing and preparing the ground for cultivation. They are worth about thirty rupees each. The value of the rice raised annually for exportation is estimated at two lakhs of rupees, or twenty thousand pounds, besides a large quantity used by the natives, and calculated at some ten rupees a-head.

The Burman has very few agricultural implements, and these are of the rudest description. A cart, plough, dah (or sword-knife), and sickle are about all he requires. The humped Indian ox is worked in the carts or drays of the country. They cost about thirty rupees a pair.

Several valuable dyes are found amongst the vegetable productions of the country, but they have not as yet formed a part of the exports.

CHAPTER XIV.

Mineral Resources of the Tenasserim Provinces.

THESE provinces possess vast and, as yet, almost untouched sources of wealth in their minerals. These are of surpassing richness and variety, and now lie absolutely neglected; while by the employment of British capital and enterprise, which so often seek employment in much less promising fields, they might be made highly remunerative to the Government, while yielding a rich return to the capitalist. Gold has been found in the alluvium of Tavoy, and indications of the precious metal are widely diffused over the provinces. Gold-washing has been tried successfully at the head of the Tavoy river. The search, however, has never been carried on below the surface, though it is highly probable, from the geological nature of the country, and the resemblance of certain districts to the auriferous regions of Australia, that, if shafts were sunk to the beds of the old creeks, remunerative gold-fields would be discovered. They could only be worked by Burmans or natives of India, in the pay of and under the direction of capitalists; for the climate would preclude the European from becoming a miner, as in California and Australia.

A much more certain investment however would doubtless be found in the valuable tin-mines of British Burmah. Of these the richest and most accessible is at Kahan, on Mergui Island, and about ten miles distant by water from the town of Mergui.*

Kahan possesses several mines of very good clean ore in great abundance, thousands

* Mergui is the most southern of the Tenasserim provinces. It is bounded on the north by the province of Tavoy, from which it is separated by the Pa Au river; on the south by the Pakchan river; on the east by that chain of mountains which divides this part of British Burmah from Siam; and on the west by the eastern side of the Bay of Bengal.

of tons of which could be had not far from the surface of the ground. It runs in thick massive veins through decomposed sandstone and clay interspersed with mica, a sure indication of its being very plentiful. Several attempts have been made from time to time to work these mines, but all have been unremunerative from want of water on the spot. The nearest creek is a few hundred yards off, and to conduct a supply of water from it to the mine should be the first consideration of the capitalist after he obtains a grant from Government; for without abundance of water, such as a good creek could supply, time and money would be thrown away. The ore yields as much as 75 per cent. of the pure metal, and costs less in smelting than that from the southern districts. Labourers may easily be obtained from villages near Kahan, as well as from Mergui; for, could they be assured the mines would be extensively worked, they would willingly settle themselves down on the spot with their families and procure from the town any necessary supplies. The place is healthy and agreeable as a residence, with good fruit-trees, and the river frontage is free from jungle. A merchant of Maulmain, with whom I conversed while there on the probable result of a shipment of tin ore to England, after a careful calculation, arrived at the conclusion that "a clear profit of 2*l.*10*s.*1¾*d.* on an actual outlay of 3*l.*0*s.*8¼*d.*" would be made.

The tin-mines further south, in the Lenyen district, are very inaccessible, and are worked by Shans and Chinese, who bring a few thousand viss* of the metal into Mergui once a-year, which finds its way into the Penang market. Life and property are unsafe in this district, the Lenyen river being often entered by boats full of Malays, who commit great depredations, and this must continue until two well-armed gun-boats are placed on the station. There are various kinds of iron ore, but the best is obtained from "Iron Island," between Tavoy and Tiger Island. Thousands of tons project out in large rocky

* A viss is equal to 360 or 365 lbs.

formations all over the island. It yields a very large per-centage of metal. For smelting purposes it could be conveyed with little difficulty or expense to Mergui, where fuel is always to be had in great abundance.*

The magnetic iron ore in the neighbourhood of Tavoy I have already alluded to. When it is further considered that coal is obtainable at no greater distance than Mergui, and that water-carriage is available, it will readily be seen that this may yet prove a source of wealth to the capitalist.

Some good specimens of lead ore have been obtained from Mergui province. These were pronounced by Professor Oldham, the Government geologist, to be of the richest kind, and containing a large quantity of silver. A great deal of lead is also known to exist in the limestone of the provinces. A very extensive deposit of the manganese of commerce has been found on the great Tenasserim river, in the district of Mergui, and reported on by

* Private information.

Captain Tremenheere, who thinks it probable it may cover "many square miles."

In the neighbourhood of Maulmain and Tavoy a new carbonaceous mineral is said to exist. It has been analysed by Mr. Piddington, curator of the Museum of Economic Geology in Calcutta, and named by him Tremenheerite, after Captain Tremenheere, who first sent it to him. Mr. Piddington gives its analysis as follows:—

Carbon	85·7
Water and sulphur . .	4·0
Peroxide of iron . .	2·5
Earth, chiefly silica . .	7·5
	99·7
Water and loss . .	3
	100·0

Mergui possesses valuable fields of coal. The beds are very extensive, from nine to eighteen feet thick and about sixteen feet from the surface. The principal mine is some ninety miles up the great Tenasserim river, to which tramways could be constructed. The coal should be floated down the river on bamboo rafts, which could then be sold. This mine was worked some years ago by the Government, but in consequence of improper management it did not prove remunerative. Cannel and other coals also exist in the province of Mergui.

CHAPTER XV.

Flora of the Tenasserim Provinces—The Palm Tribe—The Bamboo—Wood-oil Tree—Ornamental Trees—Fruits — Mangosteen — Mango — Dorian —Plantain—Pine-apple—Oranges—Jack—Cereal Grasses—Timber Trees.

THE flora of these provinces may vie with that of any part of the world. Some of the flowering trees and shrubs that here grow wild are known and highly prized in our English conservatories. Dr. Griffith, during a fourteen months' residence in the country, collected 1,700 different species of plants. The noble and graceful palm-tribe are found in great variety. Of these the cocoa-nut palm (*cocus nucifera*) is one of the most useful and widely diffused. The milk from the nut is a cooling and acceptable beverage in a tropical climate. The betel-palm (*areca catechu*) is very highly esteemed by the Burmans, on account of the nut it produces, which is universally used for chewing with the green leaf of the piper betel, or betel vine, one of the pepper-worts. These graceful trees are generally seen in small groves; each slender stem glancing upwards, straight as an arrow, and crowned by a number of short fronds.

The palmyra palm (*borassus flabelliformis*) is a remarkable looking tree. Its shaft often rises to a great height, and then sends out large rayed leaves, which almost invariably throw their shadow on the pagoda, the temple, or the kyoung; for the Burmans plant these trees in the immediate vicinity of religious edifices. A most useful tree or plant to the Burmans is the nipa, or water-palm, which grows on the banks of the rivers, particularly in Tavoy province. It bears a great resemblance to the cocoa-nut palm without its stem, as if the top, with the fronds, had been cut off, and then planted in the ground. Its roots bind together the soil on the sides of the rivers that would otherwise be washed away by the ebb and flow of the tides. The leaf is used universally for thatching purposes; the juice is converted into toddy, molasses, or vinegar, whilst its fruit is eaten when ripe, and the flower is made into a preserve; even the branches are useful as fuel.

The light graceful spear-leaved bamboo, about which the fire-flies may be seen hovering on a dark night, is one of the most valuable productions of nature to the natives of a tropical climate. Bound together by the cane or rattan, it forms the framework of a Burman's house, and he turns it to a thousand uses. The principal varieties are the thorny bamboo (*bambusa spinosa*), the gigantic bamboo (*bambusa gigantea*), and the Penang or China bamboo (*bambusa nana*).

The wood-oil tree (*dipterocarpus lævis*), though not esteemed as a timber tree, is very valuable on account of the oil it yields so freely. It grows on the banks of the higher Salween, and attains the height of one hundred and fifty or even two hundred feet in some instances, with a circumference of from eight to twelve feet. To extract the oil the Burman makes an excavation in the trunk about one foot square, and in this he lights a fire. The oil flows out very plentifully, and is collected in earthen pots. Dr. Helfer states that one trunk will produce thirty or forty gallons every season without injuring the tree. This oil has been found to be identical in its chemical properties and medicinal effects with the balsam copaiva.

From a weed (*blumea grandis*), very common throughout the provinces, a vegetable production is obtainable. Some specimens were sent to Calcutta, and of these it was reported, "that in its refined form it is identical in all its properties with Chinese camphor." As this plant is very abundant, it might doubtless be turned to good account.

The pa-douk (*pterocarpus Indicus*), a highly ornamental evergreen tree with bright yellow papilonaceous flowers, which are very fragrant, exudes a gum, which Dr. Morton found to be identical in its medicinal qualities with the gum kino of the pharmacopæia; hence it is sometimes spoken of by Mason as the "gum-kino tree."* As it is one of the most abundant trees in the Tenasserim provinces the gum might be exported in any quantity. The liquid amber tree also grows in this part of Burmah. The nutmeg tree (*myristica moschata*) is cultivated with success. Nux vomica is found in the neighbourhood of Maulmain. The bamboo fungus is a specific for worms, and has been introduced into European practice. The cutch (*acacia catechu*) is an indigenous tree, and is used by the natives with the betel-nut. The cashew tree yields a fine white gum, like gum arabic, and which has been pronounced as not inferior to it in virtue or quality.

The true arrow-root (*maranta arundinacea*) is not indigenous, but it has been introduced, and grows remarkably well, so that its cul-

* "Mason's Natural Productions of Burmah;" a work published at the Maulmain missionary press, and of which I have availed myself to a considerable extent in this and the following chapters.

tivation might be carried on very profitably. The climate is, however, quite too wet for the English potato.

The first of the flowering and ornamental trees of these provinces, and, indeed, of India beyond the Ganges, is the *Amherstia nobilis*. Dr. Wallich found it growing near Trockla, on the Salween, and he named it after the lady of the governor-general of India at that time, the Earl of Amherst. It does not grow to a great height, but is a very fair sized tree. From its branches hang splendid flowers, of a brilliant red and yellow colour, on a slender stem often more than a yard long. Several of these magnificent trees may be seen in the compounds at Maulmain and Tavoy. I brought two young *Amherstias* to England in a glass-case with every success. During the voyage they threw out leaves and grew considerably; but their value in the home market is now but trifling, though a few years ago large sums were given for this beautiful exotic.

There are two species of *mesua* in the

provinces—a beautiful evergreen tree. Its flower is white with yellow stamens; and under one of these trees the Burmans say their next Boodh, Aree-ma-taya, will appear.*

The nodding clerodendron (*clerodendron nutans*) is found in the mountain glens of Tavoy and Mergui. It is one of the most elegant of shrubs, The flowers are white, "tinged with rose, but nearly white, growing in long panicles at the extremities of the branches, from which they make a graceful curve, and hang down perpendicularly, from ten to fifteen inches, like an inverted cone; so that the soft green foliage seems canopied with rosy-white veils."†

The magnolia tribe is represented by the champac (*michelia champaca*), and the Burman maidens are fond of mingling its rich orange blossoms with their dark tresses.

The large pink-flowered knotty cassia, the splendid orange-flowered buteas, the white-flowered drooping barringtonia, the fragrant

* Mason. † Ibid.

tabernæmontana, the curious gloriosa, the large blue-flowered thunbergia, and a hundred others too numerous to mention, grow here in wild luxuriance. A very common weed on waste ground, and also in gardens, is the *mimosa sensitiva*, which shrinks from the slightest touch, bending to the ground and closing its leaves with singular rapidity. It is to this plant that Longfellow alludes in those beautiful lines :—

As, at the tramp of a horse's hoof on the turf of the Prairies,
Far in advance are closed the leaves of the shrinking mimosa,
So, at the hoof-beats of fate, with sad forebodings of evil,
Shrinks and closes the heart, ere the stroke of doom has attained it.

That beautiful tribe, the orchids, are found in great variety in these provinces. More than fifty different species have been already described.

Of the table fruits indigenous in this part of Burmah, the mangosteen (*garcinia mangostana*) holds the first place, and is truly a delicious fruit. Inside the dark red case a delicate white juicy pulp is found, of most exquisite flavour. It is cultivated in the province of Mergui, and does not flourish further north. Those grown in Tavoy are very small, but of excellent flavour.

The mango, of which there are two species (*mangifera indica* and *sylvatica*), is also a very fine-flavoured fruit of an oblong shape. It is in season during the hottest part of the year. The inferior kinds have a strong flavour of turpentine.

A most extraordinary fruit is the dorian, (*durio zibethinus*). The stranger generally finds the smell quite enough to deter him from eating it; nevertheless many Europeans become exceedingly partial to it, and with the natives it is esteemed the queen of fruits. One taste was for me quite sufficient, and I at once concluded that the natives were quite welcome to my share of this most fetid fruit.

The staple fruit of the country is the plantain or banana (*musa paradisiaca*), of which there is a constant succession all the year round. There are many varieties of plantain, and the flavour varies a good deal. Some are insipid, but others have a slightly acid flavour, which renders them very agreeable. It is a wholesome fruit, plentiful, and a great boon to the natives.

The pine-apple (*ananas sativus*), when in season, is a delicious and abundant fruit, and they are sold at the rate of four for three-halfpence, and even cheaper. The lichi (*nephelium lichi*) has been introduced, but is not yet at all plentiful. Oranges are by no means scarce, but maintain a high price. Limes are also cultivated. A very common fruit is the jack (*artocarpus integrifolius*); but, though invaluable to the natives, it is never seen on the table of Europeans. It is decidedly a disagreeable fruit, if indeed it deserves that name at all. These are the principal fruits that the stranger will find in the Tenasserim provinces.

English vegetables are scarce, and little cultivated—a few small potatoes are sometimes to be procured; but the climate is too wet for the root to attain any perfection. The sweet potato, and a dark purple yam,* are used a good deal as substitutes. Of the cereal grasses rice is the principal; and of this there are several varieties.

Several trees and plants produce dyes of various colours. The celebrated shan black dye is produced by a species of ebony (*diospyros mollis*). The ruellia is a low plant, which yields a blue dye, not inferior, it is said, to that procured from the true indigo plant. From the Mergui red-wood a valuable dye is obtained "The wood of the jack, the root of the pyschotria, the bark of the gamboge trees, the flowers of the buteas, the rind of the Bengal quince, and the leaves of the memecylon and the touk-yat, all produce bright yellow dyes."

The true caoutchouc tree of Assam has been introduced, and flourishes well.

First amongst the timber-trees of the provinces stands of course the noble teak tree

* The skin is purple, but the inside, when cooked, is as white as the potato.

(*tectona grandis*), of which mention has already been made. This tree possesses an essential oil, which preserves it, in a great degree, from the ravages of the white ant, that pest of tropical countries. It is also one of the most, if not the most, durable of woods.

The iron-wood tree, one of the acacia tribe, is also very durable. There are several species of ebony. The wood of the pa-douk, or *pterocarpus*—a tree I have already spoken of—bears a great resemblance to mahogany; and Mason in one place calls it Tenasserim mahogany. The Tavoy red-wood looks well made into furniture. Another valuable timber-tree is the *shorea robusta*. The hopea tree (*hopea odorata*) is highly prized for boat-building, and also for house-building purposes. It is indigenous in the southern provinces.

Captain Salter was, I believe, the first to discover a pine-tree, which grows in large forests eastward of the Thoung-yeen River,

and is called in consequence "*pinus Salteri.*"*
It is a heavy red wood, bearing a great resemblance to the Riga pine, and grows to the height of fifty or sixty feet, with a diameter of two feet, and sometimes more.

Altogether there are more than one hundred different kinds of valuable timber-trees in the Tenasserim provinces, all of which it would be tedious to mention.

* Mason says that Captain Latter first visited the locality where the tree is indigenous, and he calls it *Pinus Latteri.*

CHAPTER XVI.

Zoology of the Tenasserim Provinces—Carnivorous Mammalia, &c.

WITHIN the last fifteen or twenty years a very much more correct and intimate knowledge of the zoology of this part of British Burmah has been obtained, and many of the species have been identified by Mr. Blyth, Curator of the Museum of the Asiatic Society.

Of the carnivorous mammalia, of which between twenty and twenty-five species are known to exist in the Tenasserim provinces, the royal tiger (*tigris regalis*) may be placed at the head of the list. This is a truly formidable animal, and, as it abounds in every part of the country, the traveller in the jungles has to be ever on his guard. Leopards are said to be more numerous even than tigers, and ascending a tree is no protection against them; for they will run up with all the ease and agility of a cat. The black leopard (*felis melas*) is often met with. The leopard-cat is a very beautifully-marked animal. Tiger-cats are plentiful in the jungles, and sometimes pay a visit to the towns. When I was at Maulmain one was caught in a dry well close to the house in which I was residing. There are two or three other animals of the genus *felis*. The pig-bear (*arctonyx collaris*) is met with in the southern provinces; and, in the north, the monkey-tiger, which animal was first discovered in Malacca not many years ago: it is about the size of a small monkey. Otters are numerous in the streams. One species of wild dog, and two of the civet-cat, the three-striped paguma, three species of paradoxure, and an animal Mason calls the Tenasserim ichneumon (*urva cancrivora*), in contra-distinction to the genuine ichneumon, also exist.

There are six species of pachydermata, or

thick-skinned animals, to be found in the forests of the Tenasserim provinces. At the head of these stands the elephant *(elephas Indicus)*. They are numerous in some parts of the country, but do not generally interfere with or attack man unless provoked to do so. Their blowing and heavy tramp may be heard at a considerable distance. "Karens tell us that if one be wounded and not killed he immediately retreats, but, as soon as he feels the smart of his wound, he turns and rushes upon his antagonist with terrible fury. One of the best Karen marksmen I ever knew perished in this way. He shot and wounded but did not kill the elephant, which immediately ran away. His companions, knowing the habits of the animal, scattered themselves, but this man kept his ground, in confidence that he would be able to reload, and renew the attack when it returned; but, before his gun was loaded, the enraged elephant was upon him, and instantly trampled him to death."* I have already

* Mason.

spoken of the services of these powerful and sagacious animals in the timber-trade of the country, in the forests of the interior, and in the timber-yards of Maulmain.

A small black species of wild hog *(sus Indicus)* is very numerous, and commits devastations in the paddy fields.

There would appear to be no less than three distinct species of the rhinoceros. "The common single-horned rhinoceros is very abundant. Though often seen on the uninhabited banks of large rivers, as the Tenasserim, they are fond of ranging the mountains, and I have frequently met with their wallowing-places on the banks of mountain streams, two or three thousand feet above the plains. They are as fond of rolling themselves in mud as a hog or a buffalo. The Karens, when travelling, have quite as much fear of a rhinoceros as they have of a tiger. When provoked, the rhinoceros, they say, pursues his enemy most unrelentingly and with indomitable perseverance. If to escape his rage the huntsman retreats to a tree, the beast, it is said, will take his stand beneath the tree for three or four days in succession, without once leaving his antagonist." *

The double-horned smooth-skinned rhinoceros is also met with. The third species is what the Karens call the fire-eating rhinoceros, and which Mason supposes to be identical with the Javanese animal of that name. It appears to be excited by the sight of fire, to which it rushes with mad impetuosity.

The Malay tapir *(tapirus Malayanus)*, exists in the interior of the Tavoy and Mergui provinces, and it appears to be a harmless animal.

There are, in the country, eleven species of the *ruminantia*, or animals that chew the cud. Of these the deer tribe are very numerous. The chevrotain is a little deer about the size of a large hare. The same animal is found at Penang, where it is much more plentiful.

The barking-deer is very widely diffused over the provinces, and is frequently seen in

* Mason.

the neighbourhood of Maulmain and Tavoy. "It uses its horns," says Mason, "with great effect when brought to bay, and, according to a Karen fable, the tiger will not attack it. In ancient times, the story goes, when all animals had the power of speech, the tiger said to the barking-deer, 'O! barking deer, what is the use of thy horns? It seems to me they would be in my way.' The barking-deer answered, 'A single push of my horns will make the eye of my antagonist start from its socket.' On hearing this the tiger was afraid, and never after attempted to devour the barking-deer."

The hog-deer *(cervus porcinus)* is found on the plains north and east of Maulmain, and on the large islands south of Tavoy. They are easily brought to a stand by the beating of bells, gongs, and kettles, and the huntsman then shoots them at his convenience.

There is also the rusa deer, the brow-antlered rusa, and the goat-antelope.

The gaur, a bison-like animal, is seen in large droves; also a wild ox or cow (*bos sondaicus*) abounds in the uninhabited parts of the country.

The zebu or small Indian ox, with a hump, is domesticated and much used for draught. The buffalo is also domesticated, and employed by the Burmans in the tillage of the paddy-fields, where it may be seen dragging the plough through the oozy soil, or wallowing in the soft mud in which it delights. It is a huge unwieldy animal of a dark slate-colour and almost hairless skin. Its enormous head and huge retreating horns give it a ferocious appearance; indeed, many of them are very fierce, and their temper at the best of times uncertain. They sometimes have fights in the open fields, and these are generally much more obstinate than when they are brought together for the purpose in the manner I have described elsewhere. This animal bears no resemblance to the American "buffalo," which, as is well known, is not, strictly speaking, a buffalo but a bison.

Two species of the *cetacea* or whale tribe, and a species of porpoise, frequent the shores. The *quadrumana*, or monkey tribe, of which there are five species in the Tenasserim provinces, are exceedingly numerous. I have seen them by hundreds springing from tree to tree in their native jungles.

The white-handed gibbon, or long-armed ape (*grand gibbon*), abounds in the interior, and their wailing cry is heard most frequently at the break of day. The most numerous species in the provinces, however, is the fisher-monkey (*inuus ceropithecus*). It lives chiefly on small crabs and shell-fish, although it is fond of fruit and eats it greedily when it comes in its way. Mason thinks that "the apes that Solomon's fleet brought from Ophir were probably monkeys of the genus to which this species belongs." This I fear Solomon only could determine. The coaly-monkey, the long-haired pig-tailed monkey, and the white-eyelid monkey are also met with. The lemur, or Bengal sloth (*lemur tardigradus*), is also seen occasionally.

Of the *cheiroptera*, or bat tribe, four species have been identified. The flying-fox (*pteropus edulis*) is a large bat, measuring from three to four feet. It commits great depredations on the fruit, and may often be seen hanging on the tops of palmyra palms.

In the limestone caves the cave-bat may be seen by thousands. There is also the horseshoe or leaf-nosed bat, and the small or domestic bat, which latter infests houses to a great extent, getting into the roofs, and there creating so disagreeable an odour that a dwelling so beset is often uninhabitable until they have been cleared away.

Three genera of *insectivora*, or insect-eaters, have been found in the provinces. There is the Javanese sapaia, the musk-shrew, and the gymnura. Of the *rodentia*, or gnawing animals, fifteen species have been discovered. There is the two-coloured squirrel (*sciurus bicolor*), sometimes called the giant squirrel, which is as large as a cat; the golden-backed squirrel (*sciurus chrysonotus*), the large and small flying-squirrel, and several others.

The bandicoot rat commits depredations in the fowl-houses, and the common brown rat infests the dwelling-houses in great numbers. Two species of porcupine have been described, and one animal, the pangolin, represents in this part of the world the edentata or toothless animals.

CHAPTER XVII.

Ornithology of the Tenasserim Provinces—Thirty species of Rapacious Birds—Vultures—Eagles, &c.—Birds with a notch in their bills—Bulbouls—Broadbills, &c.—The Paradise Edolius—King-crow—Thrushes—Mango-bird—Oriole—Conic-billed Birds—Crows—Pies—Mynahs—Starlings—Finches—Hornbills, &c.—Habits of the Crows—Black Mynah as a talking-bird—Habits of the Hornbill—Scansores or Climbing Birds—Parrokeets—Woodpeckers—The Crow-pheasant—Suctorial Birds—Wide-mouthed Birds—Bee-eaters—Rollers—King-fishers, &c.—Gallinaceous Birds—Peacocks—Pheasants—Jungle-fowl, &c.—Wading-birds—Herons, &c.—The White Paddy-bird—Swimming-birds—Wild Ducks—Teal—Pelicans, &c.

PERHAPS there is no part of the world where the feathered tribes are more numerous and varied than in the Tenasserim provinces; but it is only within the last few years that any exact information has been obtained of the ornithology of the country;

and here again the labours of Mr. Blyth, in examining and arranging the collections of others, have been very valuable.

The *raptores*, or rapacious birds, are represented by about thirty species of vultures, eagles, kites, buzzards, harriers, falcons, hawks, gos-hawks, fish-hawks, and owls.*

Of the *dentirostres*, or birds with a notch in the bill, there are shrikes, bulbouls, thrushes, babblers, orioles, stonechats, warblers, wagtails, fruit-eaters, fly-catchers, and broodbills.

A bird that I frequently noticed flying from tree to tree in the compounds at Tavoy was the paradise edolius, (*edolius paradiseus*, or *edolius cristatellus*). Its plumage is jet-black, and is remarkable from its having two very long tail-feathers barbed at the extremity, and which at a distance occasionally give the appearance of a small bird flying after it. "The loud, flute-toned edolius," says Mason, "might be termed the Tenasserim nightingale, for it is considered

* Mason.

by the Karens as the sweetest singer of their forests, and it seems to delight in cheering them at eventide. There was an old friend that used to come at sunset every evening, and perch upon a guava bough near my dwelling in Dongyan; and there it would sit and pour forth one incessant stream of melody for half-an-hour at a time."

The king-crow is a bird not unlike the edolius, and derives its name from its habit of chasing away the crows.

Of the bulboul, that bird of poetic fame, there are several varieties; but the pink-eared bulboul is the species most common in the provinces, especially in the neighbourhood of Tavoy.

There are several species of thrushes, which are amongst the best songsters the country can boast of. The mango-bird (*oriolus melanocephalus*), or black-headed oriole, has a fine mellow note, and its plumage, with the exception of the head, is of a bright yellow.

There are two species of wagtail; one of

which, the water-wagtail, very much resembles the English bird of that name.

The *conirostres*, or conic-billed birds, are numerous, and include the crows, pies, mynahs, starlings, finches, sparrows, buntings, larks, and hornbills.

The common India black crow (*corvus culminatus*) is the most numerous of the birds of the country. They abound everywhere—in towns, villages, markets, compounds, and even in houses; which latter they enter whenever they can get an opportunity, particularly at meal-time, when they are ever on the watch, and pounce upon any eatable that falls in their way. They are most inveterate thieves. As you sit in the verandah in the early morning taking your coffee before walking, if your attention be diverted for a moment your toast takes to itself wings and flies away as fast as a crow can carry it. The fruit-women coming into town with loads of fruit on their heads, have to wield a stick in one hand to keep off these unwelcome customers, who alight on the baskets and eat from them, if allowed—a scene that recalls to memory certain passages of holy writ.

There are several varieties of the mynah, The black mynah (*gracula religiosa*), which has a yellow band on the head, is valued on account of the facility with which it learns to talk. Ten and twelve rupees, and more, is a price often asked for this bird.

The pied starling (*sturnus contra*) is very common in the compounds of Tavoy, where it may be seen following a horse or ox as it grazes, and picking up worms and insects within an inch of its mouth.

The Indian sparrow (*passer Indicus*) is almost as common as the crow. It so closely resembles the European sparrow that it was at one time supposed to be identical with that bird; but Mr. Blyth now considers it a distinct species.

The stranger is sometimes startled during his country rambles by an extraordinary rushing noise, which he soon perceives proceeds from a large and most remarkable bird, several of which are sweeping through the air over his head. This is the concave hornbill (*buceros cavatus*).

The climbing-birds are represented by parrakeets, lorikeets, woodpeckers, barbets, creepers, and cuckoos.

The black-billed parrakeet commits great devastations upon the paddy-fields.

The smallest bird of the parrot tribe is the red-rumped lorikeet. "Its Burman name signifies "headlong," from its habit of suspending itself from the tree head foremost, like a bat."

There are several species of woodpecker and barbet. A black cuckoo (*endynamys orientalis*) is sometimes seen. The bird known by the name of the crow-pheasant (*centropus Phillipensis*) also belongs to the cuckoo tribe.

Of the *tenuirostres*, or suctorial birds, there are honey-suckers, sun-birds, and hoopoes.

The *fissirostres*, or wide-mouthed birds, include bee-eaters, rollers, kingfishers, trogons, nightjars, swifts, and swiftlets. A beautiful blue kingfisher is often seen in the gardens of Tavoy. The swallow, that builds the edible nests which are found in considerable numbers on the Moscos, are very numerous in the limestone caves and islands on the coast of Tavoy. The bird-nest monopoly is rented annually to the Chinese by the Government.

The *rasores*, or gallinaceous birds, are represented in the Tenasserim provinces by peacocks, pheasants, wild-fowls, partridges, three-toed quails, green pigeons, rock-pigeons, and turtle-doves.

Very handsome peacocks inhabit the Burman jungles. The Burmans have a saying (Mason tells us) that wherever there are peacocks there are tigers.

The jungle-fowl, that is found so plentifully in the forests, appears to be identical with our domestic bird of the same name.

The Burman wood-cutters always put a jungle-fowl in their boat when going to the forests; and, using this as a decoy-bird, they entrap the wild ones, which are very numerous. There are several species of pigeons, and the plaintive coo of the turtle-dove is almost as constant as the patter of the rain in the wet season. The *grallatores*, or wading-birds, are widely distributed, and include herons, bitterns, demi-egrets, adjutants, cranes, ibises, open-beaks, rails or coots, water-hens, snipes, sand-pipers, oyster-catchers, snippets, turnstones, and plovers.

The white paddy-bird (*ardea alba*) is a beautiful white bird of the heron species, and may be observed skimming over the bright green paddy-fields, or flying along the banks of the rivers.

After dark the night-heron, whose cry so much resembles the bellowing of a cow that it is called by the Burmans the "cow-bird," is frequently heard.

The adjutant (*ciconia argala*) is common in the province of Amherst, where it builds amongst the limestone rocks.

Snipe (*scolopax heteruna*) abound in the neighbourhood of Tavoy, and may often be shot in the compounds of the town itself: they afford capital shooting to the sportsman.

The *natatores*, or swimming-birds, are re-represented by wild ducks, teal, pelicans, snake-birds, cormorants, sea-swallows, gulls, and scissor-bills. Both the naturalist and the sportsman will find an extensive field for the exercise of their respective pursuits in this part of the British possessions of the East.

CHAPTER XVIII.

Fish found in the waters of the Tenasserim Provinces—Perch—Indian Whiting—Mullet—Mango-fish—Carp family—Prawns of enormous size—Reptiles—Tortoise tribe—Two species of Crocodile—One of these identical with the Crocodile of the Nile—Natives often carried off by them—House-lizards—The Touktay—The little Geckos—Burman legend about them—Poisonous Serpents—Innocuous Serpents—Karen legend about the Python and poisonous Serpents—Entomology of the Provinces—The Lac Insect—Blister-fly—Beetles—Their Wing-cases used as Ornaments—Phantom Insects—White Ants—Their habits—Butterflies.

THE waters of the Tenasserim provinces are plentifully supplied with fish; but there would appear to be few new species. Of the large-scaled fish there are perch, the larger kind often measuring two feet in length. Besides this, the *macroleptes* include, on this coast, the cockup, bandfish, umber, Indian whiting, mullet, mango-fish, king-fish, climbing-perch, and snakeheads. The climbing-perch is a small fish which has the power of climbing up out of the water on the roots of trees, and which will make its way, the Karens say, a quarter of a mile.*

The *microleptes*, or small-scaled fish, on the Tenasserim coast, are the Indian mackarel or tunny, ophidians, long-snouts, dories, pomphrets, ribbon-fish, flat-heads, gobies, amblyopus-suckers, and periophthalmi.

Of the carp family there are numerous species, such as cirrins, labeo, barbels, breams, sustomus, perilamps, opsarions, bacailas, gudgeons, white-fish, and loaches.

There are more than thirty different species of cat-fish; tortoise-formed fishes are represented by sea-porcupines and fishing-frogs.

Prawns, the size of small lobsters, are constantly brought to table at Maulmain and Tavoy.

The reptiles of the Tenasserim provinces are very numerous. Of the tortoise tribe there are land-tortoises, marsh-tortoises, river-tortoises, and sea tortoises or turtles.† "Two species of crocodile," says Mason, "inhabit

* Mason. † Ibid.

our rivers and sea-shores, both of which are usually denominated alligators; but alligators are peculiar to America, and a glance at the scaly ridge on the back of the hind legs of the Tenasserim reptiles is sufficient to distinguish them from the alligators, which have the hind legs rounded."

One of the species of crocodile in the rivers is identical with the common crocodile of the Nile, "the leviathan of the book of Job."*

There are three or four species of the gecko or house-lizard; the largest of these is called *touktay* by the Burmans, from its peculiar cry, which bears a great resemblance to the striking of a cuckoo-clock. The natives avoid it as a noxious reptile, and certainly it is very unsightly; but it is said to be useful in destroying rats. The pretty little gecko or lizard (*hemidactylus coctæi*), so common in all Burman houses, is perfectly harmless, and its curious human-like cry resounds from every creek and cranny. Numbers are seen on every ceiling, and occa-

* Mason.

sionally they drop off on the table. The Burmans have a legend that these little creatures were men during a former state of existence, who for their crimes have been changed into their present shape, and that their cry is intended as a warning to those who hear them to lead a good life and avoid a similar fate. The spider of the English bible is supposed to have been a small gecko, closely allied to this species.

There are several species of the monitor or varan, and also several members of the iguana tribe. Poisonous serpents are numerous, but few instances occur of people being bitten by them. The smallest poisonous serpent in the provinces is the *elaps*, and the Burmans believe it has the power of re-producing itself, like the hydra of antiquity.

There are two species of the *bungarus* and two or three of the *hamadryad*. The dusky hamadryad is said to grow to the length of ten or twelve feet and in colour is nearly black. It is a very fierce serpent, and when disturbed will pursue its enemy.

The smallest of the innocuous serpents is the burrowing blind-worm or slow-worm. The natives regard it as poisonous, and can hardly be convinced to the contrary.

The python (*python reticulatus*) is a very large serpent, measuring eighteen feet and upwards. "The Karens have an apophthegm," says Mason, "that the largest python can swallow a full-grown buck rusa, horns and all, without inconvenience. They are often seen coiled up among the branches of trees, on the banks of streams in the interior, where they are frequently noosed by the Karens, who regard them as valuable food. I have seen a Karen seize one nine feet long by the tail in the water, and with the aid of his associates succeed in capturing him.

"According to a Karen legend, all the poisonous serpents derive their virulence from the python, which, though innocuous now, was originally the only one that was venomous. In those days he was perfectly white; but, having seduced away a man's wife, Aunt Ee (Eve?), he made her, while she was in his den, weave figures on his skin in the forms which are now seen. At that time, if he bit the footstep of a man in the road, such was the virulence of his poison that the man died, how far soever that man might have passed from the bitten track. The python had not, however, any ocular demonstration of the fact, so he said to the crow, 'Crow, go and see whether people die or not when I bite the foot-track.' The crow went to the neighbourhood of a Karen cabin, and found the people, as is their custom at funerals, laughing, singing, dancing, jumping, and beating drums. He therefore returned to the python, and told him, that, so far from his efforts producing death, on the contrary they produced joy. The python was so angry when he heard this, that he ascended a tree, and spit up all his venom; but other creeping things came and swallowed it, and people die of their malignancy to this day.

"The python made them promise, however, not to bite without provocation. The cobra said, 'If there be transgression so as to dazzle my eyes, to make my tears fall seven times in one day, I will bite.' So said the tiger and others,* and they were allowed to retain their poison. But the water-snake and frog said they would bite with or without cause, as they liked, so the python drove them into the water, where their poison melted away, and their bite became harmless. The tree, however, from which the python spit up his venom, became deadly, and its juice is used to this day for the purpose of poisoning arrows.

"The gall-bladder of the python is much sought after for its medicinal virtues, which are in great repute, especially among Karens."

There are two species of rat-snake—the striped rat-snake (*coluber radiatus*) and the brown-green rat-snake† (*coluber korros*)—and

* The Karens believe that the bite of the tiger is poisonous, like that of a venomous serpent.

† "Under certain circumstances," Mason observes, "the Burmans say the bite of this serpent is fatal. These are five—gnang-soung, loo-soung, young-soung, lan-soung,

the like number of the *tropidonotus*. The ribbon-snake, the variegated tree-snake, and several species of water-snake, complete the list of this class of serpents.

Of the frog-tribe Mason mentions the tiger-frog and two species of tree-frog, but he omits the bull-frog; numbers of which I have seen taken from empty wells, and their croaking it is not easy to mistake.

To the enthusiastic entomologist these provinces, in common with every tropical country, present a wide and almost unexplored field for the study of his favourite department of natural history. "Insects form," says Mason, "by no means the least important portion of our natural productions.

ne-soung: 'snake-oblique, man-oblique, turban-oblique, road-oblique, and sun-oblique.' That is, if the snake approaches a man with its head askance, as this snake is always said to do, and the man look at it askance, and if his turban be put askance, and he be moving on the road askance, and the sun be askance descending in the heavens—when these five circumstances meet, if the snake bite, which by the way is always very improbable, death will certainly ensue!"

The lac insect, the blister-fly, the honey-bee, and the silk-moth, are important for their utility—the green beetles, the fire-flies, and the butterflies, for their beauty—the white ants, the blights, and the caterpillars, for their predatory habits; and the gnats, the mosquitoes, the gadflies, the ticks, the bugs, the fleas, the scorpions, and centipedes, for their annoyances to man."

Beetles are in great variety. There are, "tiger-beetles, ground-beetles, bombardier-beetles, whirling water-beetles, mimic-beetles, stag-beetles, scareb-beetles, atlas-beetles, chaffer-beetles, chameleon green beetles, click-beetles, glow-worms, fire-flies, floral beetles, blister-flies, scale-like beetles, long-snouted beetles, capricorn-beetles, tortoise-beetles, and ladybird-beetles." *

The chameleon-beetle "is a species of *buprestis*, an elegant insect, with one uniform hue of variable copper and green, burnished with transparent golden bronze. The elytra or wing-cases of these 'living jewels' are in

* Mason.

great demand by the Sgau Karen maidens for necklaces and chaplets, and, wreathed with a few wild flowers, around their ebon locks, they have really an appearance of elegance. There is a glow-worm often seen that bears a strong resemblance to its English namesake. The beautiful fire-flies, which swarm about the bushes on a dark night, are a species of glowworm, and they emit their light from the last segment of the abdomen."* These flies show a partiality for particular trees.

Of that extraordinary tribe known as phantom insects there are several species, such as the walking-leaf insect *(phyllium)*. It is two or three inches long, and resembles a green leaf. The natives believe it to be a true leaf changed into an insect. The walking-lichen insect and the walking-stick insect both resemble the objects implied by their names. The latter is nearly a foot long. There are several species of grasshoppers and locusts.

* Mason.

The nerve-winged insects found in the provinces are termites or white ants, damsel-flies or dragon-flies, and ant-lions.

The most remarkable of these are the white ants, so unfavourably known to all who have lived in India and other countries where they abound. Nothing is safe from their ravages; books, clothes, and every perishable article, are destroyed wholesale, without considerable care. On my first arrival in the country I had an opportunity of witnessing another annoyance proceeding from the same insect. At the commencement of the rains they become winged, and as soon as the lights are produced in an evening they swarm round them in such numbers as to drive away every one from the table.

The habits of the ant-lions (*myrmeleonidæ*) are exceedingly curious. Their pit-falls, in the form of inverted cones, serve as traps to the unwary insects that travel in their vicinity. Just within these the ant-lion lies concealed, and seizes its prey as soon as it falls to the bottom of the hole.

The gauze-winged insects are represented by gall-insects, ichneumon-flies, wasps, stinging ants, common ants, hornets, and bees.

The butterflies of Burmah are beautiful in the extreme. A rare and handsome butterfly is the priam *(ornithoptera priamus)*. Its wings are black and green. The atlas-moth measures in the smallest specimens eight or nine inches across its wings.

There is a winged bug, with an offensive odour similar to the bed bug. The latter has existed in Burmah from time immemorial, and few native houses are without it.

Of the *diptera*, or two-winged insects, the mosquitoes are the most numerous and troublesome. House-flies do not exist in any numbers, and are not as troublesome as in England during a hot summer.

There are several species of spider, and the *myriapoda* are represented by several of those ugly and dangerous creatures known as centipedes, of which two or three species are common. One of these *(scolopendra phosphorea)* emits a phosphorescent light.

CHAPTER XIX.

The Boodhism of Burmah—Its leading Doctrines—The "Nats"—Method of propitiating the Wicked Nats—Gau-dă-ma—The Burman Priests or Pon-gyees—The Objects of the Brotherhood—The Ceremony of making a Pon-gyee—Government of the Kyoungs or Monasteries—The five additional Commandments incumbent on the Pon-gyees—The Practice of Confession—The Kyoungs, the National Schools of Burmah.

I HAVE already described and illustrated the religious buildings of the Burmans, and referred incidentally to their faith, but in this chapter I propose to give the reader a fuller account of that remarkable form of belief which prevails in Chĭn-India.

Burmah, from time immemorial, has been one of the strongholds of Boodhism (or Budhism), which from Bengal is spread all over Eastern Asia, including the Japanese archipelago, and numbers amongst its followers nearly one-fourth of the human race. This fact alone is sufficient to invest it with a peculiar interest, as opening an important chapter in the history of man, and illustrating a peculiar phase of the human mind. It teaches many great truths, but they are overlaid and mixed up with the grossest errors and superstitions.

The Boodhism of Burmah and farther India is identical with that of Ceylon, from whence it was derived, but differs from that of Thibet, China, and Japan.

The leading doctrines or dogmas of this creed are—1st. The eternal existence of the universe and matter; the duration, destruction, and reproduction of the world according to eternal self-existing laws. 2nd. Metempsychosis, or the transmigration of the soul of man into the bodies of different men, women, and animals, according to its merits and demerits, until at last, purified from all imperfections, it arrives at the tranquillity of "Nieban," in which the soul, delivered from all earthly toils and distractions, exists in a state of complete abstraction and absolute rest. 4th. The appearance at long and unequal intervals of mysterious and almost divine beings, called Boodhs or Budhas. A Boodh, after going through myriads of successive existences, and the practice of numberless virtues, at length becomes endowed with such a perfect knowledge of all things as to be able to enunciate a law for the salvation of mortals, and this he preaches for a longer or shorter period; at the end of which time he arrives at the state of Nieban, after which his images are worshipped by his followers. Of these beings twenty-eight have already appeared, twenty-three of them in worlds previous to the present one. In this world four have already been manifested, viz., Kan-tha-than, Gau-na-gon, Ka-tha-pa, and Gau-da-ma. The fifth, Ari-mi-day-ya, is yet to come. The first Boodh lived 80,000 years, the second 90,000, and was eighty cubits in stature.

The Commandments are—1st. Thou shalt not kill any living creature. 2nd. Thou shalt not steal. 3rd. Thou shalt not give thyself up to carnal pleasures. 4th. Thou shalt not lie. 5th. Thou shalt not drink wine or any intoxicating liquors.

Boodhists acknowledge no Supreme Being; but they hold three things as deserving the deepest veneration, viz., Pra, or Budha, his law, and the assembly of the perfect.*

They believe in four states of punishment: hell; transmigration into insects, fish, and reptiles; transmigration into animals; and the abode of the fallen Nats under Myenmo hill.

The inferior celestial regions Boodhists believe to be inhabited by "Nats," who may be likened to the fairies, gins, and devis of other countries and creeds, or even to the angels of the Christian faith. They occupy six seats or abodes of happiness. Nats "are spirits endowed with a body of so subtle and ethereal a nature, as to be able to carry themselves with an urgent rapidity from their seats to that of man, and *vice versâ*. They play a conspicuous part in the affairs

* Rev. T. Bigandet.

of this world, and are supposed to exercise a considerable degree of influence over man and other creatures. Fear, superstition, and ignorance have peopled all places with Nats. Every tree, forest, fountain, village, and town has its protecting Nat. Some among the Nats have lost their high station through misconduct, have been banished from their seats, and doomed to drag a wretched existence in some gloomy recesses. They are called wicked Nats. Their power for doing evil is supposed to be very great. Hence the excessive dread of those evil genii entertained by all Boodhists. A good deal of their commonest superstitious rites have been devised for propitiating those enemies to all happiness, and averting the calamitous disasters which they seem to keep hanging over our heads."*

The Burmans leave many offerings at certain places to propitiate the wicked Nats. In case of illness, if the remedies of the Burman doctors (and they have none worthy the

* Rev. T. Bigandet.

name) prove ineffectual, they immediately conclude that the patient is suffering from the enmity of a wicked Nat—that bugbear of the Burman imagination, and an endeavour is then made to obtain its favour by various presents. "All kinds of misfortune" says the Rev. T. Bigandet, "are attributed to the malignant interference of the evil Nats. In cases of severe illness which have resisted the skill of native medical art, the physician gravely tells the patient and relatives that it is useless to have recourse any longer to medicines, but a conjurer must be sent for to drive out the wicked spirit who is the author of the complaint. Meanwhile directions are given for the erection of a shed, where offerings intended for the inimical Nat are deposited. A female relative of the patient begins dancing to the sound of the musical instruments. The dancing goes on at first in a rather quiet manner, but it gradually grows more animated, until it reaches the acmé of animal phrensy. At that moment the bodily strength of the dancing lady becomes exhausted; she drops on the ground in a state of apparent faintness; she is approached by the conjurer, who asks her if the invisible foe has relinquished its hold of the disease. Having been answered in the affirmative, he bids the physician to give medicines to the patient, assuring him that his remedies will now act beneficially for restoring the health of the sick, since their action will meet no future opposition."

Gau-da-ma the last Boodh (or rather his image) now claims the worship of the faithful until the advent of his successor. Having during a vast number of transmigrations attained a very exalted degree of merit, he was at last born as the son of Shoodawdaneh, king of Behar in Hindostan, about the year 626 B.C. In the thirty-fifth year of his age he became a Boodh, performed numberless good actions, delivered a code of laws, passed much of his time in prayers and meditations, and finally obtained Nieban in the year 542 B.C. His images, now the objects of Boodhist adoration, crowd in great numbers the temples and other religious edifices of the Burmans. Many are of colossal stature and richly gilt. They are made of wood, metal, alabaster, and earthenware. The sayings of Gau-da-ma, reduced to writing, form the sacred book of the Burmans, which is in the Pali language. Some of the copies are very beautiful, the leaves being covered with a varnish black as jet and hard as enamel, and on these the words are emblazoned in letters of gold.

The Burman word for priest is *Pon-gyee or Phon-gyee*, meaning "great exemplar" or "great glory." In the writings of the early Portuguese authors they generally go by the name of *Talapoins*, and this term is still occasionally used by writers.

The members of this order are, however, strictly speaking, not so much priests as monks, for in an atheistical system like Boodhism the idea of a priesthood is inadmissible. The ostensible object of the brotherhood is the observance of the laws of Boodha in a more perfect manner than is possible while leading a secular life, and the attainment of a degree of excellence and sanctity that would be otherwise impossible.

The Burman pon-gyee is not charged with the moral and religious supervision of the people, and does not interfere in their religious ceremonies and worship. He renounces the world, its enjoyments and pleasures, wears a particular dress, possesses no property, but is subject to the will of his superior and the rules of his order. Nearly every Burman youth becomes the inmate of a kyoung for a longer or shorter time, and this is considered a great event in his life. His relatives and friends accompany him to the threshold of the monastery, where he bids adieu to them and the outer world. His head is shaved, his fine clothes are taken away and replaced by a loose robe of yellow; study, religious observances, and other duties connected with his new mode of life, now fill up his time. In a procession of this description ("making a pon-gyee") that I saw at Maulmain last year (1857) there were several buffoons who displayed their antics whenever the opportunity offered, as during a halt. The boy rode on a pony gaily caparisoned, surrounded by several male attendants, who held a large umbrella over his head, and he was for the time the cynosure of every eye. The object seems to be to crowd into one day the worldly pomp, excitement, and pleasure from which he is to be debarred during his monastic life. The dresses of the women on this occasion were very elaborate, and on their persons were many valuable jewels and gold ornaments. They also carried a number of baskets filled with fruit and other eatables intended as presents to the kyoung of which the youth was about to become an inmate. The young novice ministers to the wants of his superiors; and, besides the five commandments binding on all Boodhists, he must observe five others, which forbid him to eat after mid-day, to dance, sing, or play on any musical instrument, to colour his face, to stand on elevated places, to touch gold or silver. The trespassing of these may be expiated by penance; but, if the monk should violate either of those other commandments before enumerated as binding on every one, he is immediately expelled from the monastery. Those who become pon-gyees for a time only generally return to a secular life after a period of one or two years; others who remain after the age of twenty years are solemnly admitted professed members of the community, and receive the name of *Patzin.*

Every kyoung is governed by a head or superior, who regulates its affairs and attends to the moral and religious training of those placed under his direction. There are many of these religious houses in every town and village, and they are under the jurisdiction of a general superior. The ordination of pon-gyees, or the form of admission into the brotherhood which answers to it, is a very long and important ceremony. The candidate must be provided with a vessel of a truncated spheroidal form,* which he uses when, in company with other members of the

* The Latta.

kyoung, he goes his morning rounds to collect the food so freely bestowed by the people. He must also produce the yellow garments* in which he is henceforth to be clothed. Even after this solemn consecration to a monastic life the monk may be absolved from his vows and become a lay member of society; and he may be re-admitted into the order by a repetition of the forms and usages observed on the former occasion. Those who continue pon-gyees for life, or during a long period, are regarded as peculiarly holy.

The practice of confession is found to obtain amongst these Boodhist monks, though it is now less strictly observed than formerly, and in many instances has become a mere form. The virtues of humility, self-denial, and chastity are strictly inculcated. The pon-gyee shaves his head, goes bare-footed, and wholly eschews the society of women. Celibacy is indeed very strictly enjoined. The priest is not to remain under the same roof or travel in the

* Hiwaran.

same carriage or boat as women. Indeed, to such absurd lengths are these precautions carried, that the rules on this head extend even to the mother of a member of the brotherhood. "The Wini, in treating of this precept," says M. Bigandet, "extends the prohibition to one's own mother; and, even should it happen that she falls into a ditch, her son, if a pon-gyee, must not pull her out. But, in case no other aid is at hand, he may offer her his habit, or a stick, to help her out, but at the same time he is to imagine that he is only pulling out a log of wood!" The same rules apply to the intercourse of the monks with the nuns. These are comparatively few in number, but they may sometimes be observed in the streets of a Burman town. They are invariably old women, wrinkled and ugly. They are habited in loose garments of a dirty-white colour, and are generally miserable-looking objects.

The life of strict celibacy incumbent on every pon-gyee is one reason why the Christian missionaries meet with so few converts amongst the Burmans. "They have wives," they say, "possess goods, and enjoy the good things of this life." All this is, according to their deeply-rooted prejudices, quite inconsistent with the character of a holy man and spiritual guide.

A pon-gyee never returns any spoken thanks for anything that may be given him, but he is strictly forbidden to ask for what he may want. He often attains his object, however, by indirect means, and of this I met with some curious instances. At Tavoy on one occasion I accompanied a friend on a visit to a pon-gyee with whom he was acquainted. The kyoungs are always well stocked with images of Gau-da-ma of all sizes, and my companion taking a fancy to one of these asked the good father to give it to him. At first he refused, saying it was against their rules to give anything away; but he was evidently desirous that his white friend should possess the image; so after a little while he remarked that, "though he could not *give* it to his visitor, yet if the latter *took it*, and promised to make plenty of shék-ho* to it, he would offer no opposition." It was amusing to observe the struggle between his desire to make the present and his fear of violating the rule. Like the pharisees of old, it is to be feared that the yellow brotherhood too often transgress the spirit, while they observe the letter, of their commandments. On entering a monastery I have often been offered cigars and betel-nut.

The greatest respect is paid to the order by all classes of the people. Nor does this cease with the death of the pongyee; for when that event takes place he is carefully embalmed, and the rites of cremation are performed with great display, as described at page 85 *et seq*.

As I have before mentioned, the kyoungs are the national schools of Burmah, where the boys are daily taught free of all charge.

* A homage performed by raising the joined hands to the forehead and bending forwards.

Hence no male Burman is to be found without some elementary education—an example yet to be imitated by certain free and enlightened countries of the civilised world. Whatever may be the faults of the brotherhood, they doubtless confer, in this respect, an immense boon on their countrymen.

This brief account of the great monastic order of the Burmans will, I hope, give the general reader some little insight into the manners, customs, and objects of the society; and, should it be his lot some day to make acquaintance with these strange subjects of England's Queen in their own country, his having previously learned somewhat about them and their religion will not fail to add considerable interest to his intercourse with these disciples of Boodh.

CHAPTER XX.

Language and Alphabet of the Burmans—Peculiar form of the Burman character—Literature—Specimens—A Kingdom destroyed by a drop of Honey—The Rich Man's Daughter and her three Lovers—The Potter and the Washerman.

THAT great branch of the Mongolian family, which includes those nations inhabiting the south-eastern peninsula, Thibet and China, is characterised by what are termed the monosyllabic languages—languages which are without inflection, having neither conjugation nor declension, and from the simplicity or rudeness of their construction are more easily acquired by Europeans than those of Western Asia.

The vernacular tongue of the Burmans belongs to this class. As it is however difficult of pronunciation, and many words spelt exactly alike, and only differing slightly when spoken, have very opposite meanings, it is by no means so easy as might at first be supposed to one accustomed only to the grammatical and finished structure of the western languages. Those Europeans and Americans well acquainted with the Burman tongue with whom I have conversed, invariably pronounced it a difficult language to master thoroughly. I met, however, with one exception to this universal opinion, in the case of a young officer of considerable talent, who had made astonishing progress in Burmese in a short space of time; but he evidently possessed a gift for languages.

As regards its structural peculiarities, "it has no inflections, and depends almost entirely on juxta-position for the relative value of its words. Its pronouns and particles are peculiar, its idioms few and simple, its metaphors of the most obvious kind; but it is copious in terms expressive of rank and dignity, and the rank of the speaker is indicated by the peculiar phraseology which he employs. Repetitions of the same turn of expression are affected rather than shunned, and a sententious brevity and naked simplicity are the greatest beauties of which the language admits. When spoken it is even more simple than if written, the affixed particles being often omitted, so that the mere skeleton of a sentence only is presented to the hearer, the speaker, as it may be conjectured, rather hinting at his meaning than expressing it fully and distinctly, as in more perfect languages." *

It is written from left to right, but admits of no division between the words. The alphabet consists of forty-four letters, viz. thirty-four consonants and ten vowels. It has been significantly called "the round *o* language," as most of its letters are circles, or segments of circles, being in fact a circular variety of the ancient Nagri or Pali, and on the introduction of that alphabet and literature from Hindostan many terms derived from the Pali were adopted; but they remain as distinctly extraneous now as when they were first admitted. They are used in

* Craufurd.

Burman books to express certain metaphysical and pyschological doctrines appertaining to the mysteries of Boodhism, which the vernacular tongue is quite incapable of rendering.*

But, besides the vernacular tongue, the Burmans have in common with other Boodhist nations a sacred language—the language of the priests and the religious writings. This is the Pali, which bears the same relation to the common language of the Burmans as the Sanscrit does to that of the Hindoos. The Palis, according to tradition, were once a powerful nation inhabiting Bengal, Behar, and Oude, their chief city being Baliaputhra, or Balibothra, no remains of which now exist, and even the spot on which it once stood is uncertain: some supposing it to have been that now forming the site of Allahabad, while others point to the neighbourhood of Bhagulpore on the Ganges, the city and nation having both long since passed away.†

* Judson and Latter.

† Craufurd.

Printing is unknown to the Burmans, except where introduced by the missionaries; and their literature, if they can be said to have any, is composed chiefly of legends, ballads, and histories. The religious romances are compositions of a somewhat higher order. In the royal library are several thousand volumes, including works on ethics, law, history, poetry, and medicine. Some are written on sheets of ivory, the margins of which are gilt, others on fine palmyra leaves variously ornamented; but those of a common sort are made of an inferior palm-leaf, on which, as has been already mentioned, the letters are engraved with an iron stile. Books in the Pali character, which is square and angular, are often richly ornamented, and written on sheets of ivory, silver, or copper. The palmyra leaf is generally used for letter-writing, and is then made up into a circular form, and sealed or tied with tape.* In British Burmah, however, paper used for writing material by some of the

* Symes.

pon-gyees in the kyoungs, as well as by the elder pupils.*

The Damathat, which has been already alluded to as forming the Burman code of laws, may also be quoted to illustrate the spirit of Burman literature, of which, indeed, it is an important part. The following significant story is from the fourteenth volume of that great work:—

"Regarding a Case where a Kingdom was destroyed by a Drop of Honey.

"Oh excellent king! Kings, ministers, and the heads of the people must instruct and warn them that great offences may be diminished, and small offences extinguished; they shall not say, 'Oh, the case has not come before me, the people please themselves,' and thus be negligent and only enjoy themselves; for, throughout the whole succession of worlds, every Para has declared that cities and kingdoms are destroyed by enemies who, originally insignificant, have in the process

* Personal experience.

of time become powerful. As an illustration: in former times in Benares, when Brahmadat was king, he had a bramin prophet whom he consulted by day and by night. One day, seated on an exalted place, the king and the bramin were eating parched corn mixed with honey, on a beautiful white cloth; as the king was helping himself a drop of honey as large as a mustard-seed fell on the cloth; the king and the bramin both saw it: the king, maintaining his dignity, did not wipe it up, and the bramin, it being more immediately before the king, would not venture to stretch out his arm to do so: a fly came and ate it; but neither would move to drive it away: then a spider came and swallowed the fly; still, though both saw it, neither would drive it away: and after this a lizard seized and swallowed the spider: and, even then, neither drove it away: next a rat came and swallowed the lizard; still, though both saw it, neither would interfere: then a cat came and ate up the rat; then a dog attacked the cat, and the owner of the cat and dog quarrelled, and still the king and the bramin did not interfere to put a stop to it, but continued thoughtlessly to enjoy themselves. The owner of the dog went to one of the princes, and the owner of the cat to another, and when both had collected a strong party they came to blows; and then, though the king, and the bramin, and the ministers tried to quiet the disturbance, they could not, and, the strength of the parties increasing, the king, the bramin, the wealthy, and the poor were killed and destroyed: and thus the kingdom of Benares came to an end, as is well known, all through a single drop of honey. This the words of the gods of the succession of worlds, Menoo, the recluse, the son of the king of Bymahs, revealed to the great king Maha Thamadah."

To give an illustration of the spirit of "The Decisions of Princess Thoo-dhamma Isari," another Burman book, I select the following from that work.*

* Translated from the Burmese by Captain Sparks, principal Assistant-Commissioner of Arracan.

"INTRODUCTION.

"The words of kings, of nobles, of judges, and of wise men are to be likened to the stroke of a thunderbolt, to a two-edged sword cutting through a plantain-leaf, to a strong wind shaking a tree. Judges who have at heart their happiness in this world and the next should continually examine the whole of the law with a view to the destruction of evil-doers, and after inquiry into all offences great and small, according to law, should decide justly."

"THE RICH MAN'S DAUGHTER AND HER THREE LOVERS (Story 15).

"During the era of Gaunagong* there lived in Kambautsa four rich men, between whom existed a warm friendship. Three of them had each one son, whilst the fourth had an only daughter of perfect beauty, and to her each of the three young men sent a

* The twenty-fifth Boodh, who lived 30,000 years, and was thirty cubits in stature.

messenger. The first promised that if she died before she was fifteen he would perform her funeral rites with every care. To this her parents replied, 'It is well.' The second sent to say that in the above case he would collect her ashes.* To this also her parents signified their assent. The third sent to say that he would watch her tomb; to which her parents returned the same answer as before.

"The damsel did die before she had attained her fifteenth year, and her parents desired the young men to bury her as they had promised; whereupon the first performed the rites of cremation, the second collected and removed her ashes, and the third kept watch over them in the cemetery, according to their respective promises. A jagee, who had come from the Himalaya forests, happening to pass that way at the time, saw the young man keeping watch, and inquired the reason of his doing so, to which

* Literally, "carry her bones." It is the custom at Burmese funerals, after burning the corpse, to collect the remains and bury them.

he replied he was watching over the bones of the dead. 'Would you wish the dead to be restored to life?' asked the jagee, 'I would,' replied the youth; upon this the jagee restored the damsel to life in all her pristine beauty of form and feature.

"The first rich man's son said (when he saw her,) 'I bore her corpse to the funeral pile and burnt it, therefore ought she not to be mine?' the second, 'I collected her bones, ought she not to be mine?' the third, 'whilst I was watching in the cemetery she returned to life, ought she not to be mine?' 'But what is the use of disputing with each other? Let us submit to the decision of princess Thoo-dhamma Isari.' So they all three repaired to her presence and related to her the affair. When she had heard them she thus gave judgment: 'I understand this matter; one of you burnt the corpse of the damsel, and went his way: the second collected her ashes, and did likewise: but the third kept watch over her remains, although the family of a watcher in a cemetery is degraded to the seventh generation. During his watching also the damsel returned to life; therefore, as he deserted her not in death, let him be her partner in life.'"

"THE POTTER AND THE WASHERMAN.

"In the olden time, during the era of Thoo-moyd-ha,* a potter conceived an evil design against a washerman, who lived with considerable ostentation, and, being unable to bear the sight of the wealth which the latter had acquired by washing clothes, he determined to come to an open rupture with him. With this view he went to the king and said, 'Your majesty's royal elephant is black; but, if you were to order the washerman to wash it white, would you not become lord of the white elephant?'† This speech was not made from any zeal for the king's advantage, but because he thought that if the order was

* The sixteenth Boodh, who lived 90,000 years, and was eighty-eight cubits in stature.

† The white elephant is so highly prized in Burmah that it is regarded almost in the light of a deity; and the king would consider it a great calamity to be without one.

given to the washerman according to his suggestion, and the elephant should not turn white after all, the fortune of the washerman would come to an end.

"The king, on hearing the representation of the potter, took for granted it was sincere, and, being deficient in wisdom, he, without consideration, sent for the washerman and ordered him to wash the royal elephant white.

"The washerman, seeing through the potter's design, replied, 'Our art requires that, in order to bleach cloth, we should first put it in a boiler with soap and water, and then rub it well. In this manner only can your Majesty's elephant be made white.' The King considering that it was a potter's business, and not a washerman's, to make pots, called for the potter, and said to him, 'Heh, you potter, a pot is required to lather my elephant in; go and make one large enough for the purpose.' The potter on receiving this order collected together all his friends and relations; and, after they had accumulated a vast quantity of clay, he made a pot big enough to hold the elephant, which on completion he laid before the King, who delivered it over to the washerman.

"The washerman put in soap and water; but, as soon as the elephant placed his foot upon it, it broke in pieces.

"After this the potter made many others, but they were either too thick, so that the water could not be made to boil in them, or too thin, so that the first pressure of the elephant's foot smashed them to pieces. In this manner being constantly employed he was unable to attend to his business, and so he was utterly ruined. Therefore such as aim at the destruction of others will find that their weapons will fail to reach those whom they intended, and will only recoil upon their own heads. Although a person be ever so poor, he ought not to design evil against others. Men who are guilty of treacherous actions should be avoided."

Such stories, containing as they do excellent morals, are admirably adapted for the simple people for whom they are intended.

CHAPTER XXI.

Tribes inhabiting the Tenasserim Provinces—The Talaings—Selungs—Karens—Their remarkable traditions—Specimen—Curious instance of zeal outstripping knowledge amongst the Pwo Karens—Karen School at Tavoy.

Besides the true Burmans, there are several other tribes to be found scattered over the Tenasserim provinces.

The Telaings, or Moans, are descendants of the ancient Peguans, and are now so intermingled with the Burmans, whom they resemble in appearance, dress, manners, customs, and religion, that a stranger cannot distinguish one from the other. Their language, however, is different. It is said that no very friendly feeling exists between the two races, the national antipathy of former times not having yet died out.

The Toungthus, a wandering tribe, are very thinly scattered over the provinces;

their head-quarters being in Burmah proper. They call themselves *Pa-au.* Their language has some affinity with that of the *Pwo-Karens;* and they write it in the Burman character.*

In the islands of the Mergui archipelago, a poor and inoffensive people are found, known by the name of Selungs, or Salones. The Rev. Mr. Kincaid, who paid a visit to them some years ago, writes: "I am now surrounded by about three hundred souls, men, women, and children, entirely free from all religion. They have no God, no temple, no priest, no holy day, and no prayers. In their domestic habits they are free from all conventional rules. They are very poor too, having no houses, no gardens, no cultivated fields, nor any domestic animals but dogs. I never saw such abject poverty, such an entire destitution of all the comforts of life." Their food is rice and fish; the former, as well as clothes, they obtain at Mergui, where they also dispose of the sea-slugs, which it is

* Mason.

their employment to collect at low water, at the time of the north-east monsoon. During the south-west monsoon they occupy themselves in making mats. The missionaries have effected a few conversions amongst them.

But, perhaps, in some respects at least, the most interesting people inhabiting British Burmah are the Karens, a wandering race. Of these there are two distinct tribes, viz. the Pwos or Talaing Karens, and the Sgaus or Burman Karens. They are met with in every part of the country. Their languages are somewhat different, but have a common origin; and, when one is acquired, the other is easily learnt.*

"The Sgaus are remarkable," says Mason, "for the scriptural traditions that exist among them. They have traditions of the creation, the temptation, the fall, and the dispersion of nations, in prose and verse, nearly as accurate as they are found in the Bible. The following is a single specimen:—

* Mason.

Anciently God commanded, but Satan appeared, bringing destruction.

Formerly God commanded, but Satan appeared, deceiving unto death.

The woman E-u and the man Tha-nai pleased not the eye of the dragon.

The persons of E-u and Tha-nai pleased not the mind of the dragon.

The dragon looked on them; the dragon beguiled the woman and Tha-nai.

How is this said to have happened?

The great dragon succeeded in deceiving —deceiving unto death.

How do they say it was done?

A yellow fruit took the great dragon, and gave to the children of God.

A white fruit took the great dragon, and gave to the daughter and son of God.

They transgressed the commands of God, and God turned his face from them.

They transgressed the commands of God, and God turned away from them.

They kept not all the words of God—were deceived, deceived unto sickness.

They kept not all the law of God—were deceived, deceived unto death."

In consequence of these remarkable traditions, which they say are derived from a book they once possessed, but have now lost, and also the belief that this book, together with true religion, was to be restored to them by white teachers from beyond the sea, they have proved very apt disciples of the Christian missionaries established in Burmah; some of whom are especially deputed to this particular race.

We have seen that the Burmans possess a regularly organised religion—one calculated to have a very strong hold on the mind of a half-civilised and uneducated people—with temples and sacred edifices almost innumerable. But it is far otherwise with the Karens; they are not Boodhists, and, if we except the scriptural traditions so remarkably preserved among them, have no religious creed, no systematic theology or mythology, and, as a consequence, no priests, monks, nor monastic institutions.

The Burmans have ever, with a few exceptions, turned a deaf ear to the Christian teachers, whom they cannot be brought to look on as possessed of any pretension to a sacred character, inasmuch as they possess goods and houses of their own and, worst of all—most abominable of all in Burman estimation—actually have wives, and do not wholly eschew the company of women. On the other hand, the Karen Mission is one of the most successful in the world. Their language, which was merely oral, has been reduced to writing by the missionaries, and is printed in the Burman character, with some slight additions. A dictionary, grammar, and the whole Bible have been issued in the Sgau dialect.

"In the Tenasserim provinces alone (says Mason) more than fifty different villages and hamlets have been occupied for a longer or shorter period by native assistants, under the direction of the missionaries, most of whom have charge of schools.

"Owing to the erratic habits of the people

many of these stations have been abandoned for others, but the last reports show that fifteen are occupied in the provinces of Tavoy and Mergui, and about the same number in the province of Amherst. Upwards of a thousand Karens have been baptized in the southern provinces, of whom rather more than a tenth have been Pwos and the others Sgaus. According to the last report the present number of baptized converts in the Tavoy and Mergui provinces is nine hundred and thirty-three.

"About the same number have been baptized in Amherst province. The whole Karen population of these provinces does not probably exceed sixteen thousand.

"In the district of Rangoon there are about twenty out-stations, and more than a thousand Karens have been baptized, nearly all of whom have been Sgaus.

"In the districts of Bassein and Sandoway more than six thousand Karens have been baptized, of whom about three hundred have been Pwos. More than five thousand unbaptized Christians, or catechumens, are also reported from the same region.

"Thus, in less than a quarter of a century from the commencement of missionary labours among the Karens, near ten thousand persons have been baptized, and more than fifteen thousand hopefully converted. At the present time there are between ninety and one hundred out-stations scattered over an extent of country embraced in six degrees of latitude and five of longitude, at each of which are located native teachers and preachers able to expound the New Testament, and to teach the elements of knowledge usually taught in common schools in Europe and America.

"It will be observed that, in proportion to the population, a very large number of Karens have embraced Christianity in these provinces: in Tavoy and Mergui about one-sixth, and in Amherst province one-tenth."

It has been stated that comparatively few of the Pwo Karens have become Christians, and one reason is that Boodhism has gained some footing amongst them; and just in proportion as this is the case the prospect of their receiving the purer creed is lessened. When the missionaries tell the Boodhist of the true God, he asks who his father was, and many other equally absurd questions. "We know," he says, "who Gau-da-ma was, and who his parents were; but of this God of yours we know nothing." Mason, in his history of the first Karen convert, published in a missionary magazine, relates a highly amusing and characteristic instance of zeal outstripping knowledge amongst the Pwo Karens. He says: "On reaching Tamenmats, a Pwo settlement, we found one or two men who had visited Mr. Boadman in Tavoy, and returned with the report that all the people were directed by him to build zayats, and worship according to the Christian books. They had therefore built a very fine chapel, with a graduated pyramidal roof, after the model of the finest Boodhistic religious buildings. The interior had a double court, one elevated a few steps above the other, and a central room, each separated from the other by a partition of mats three or four feet high. A model of a smaller temple stood in the central sanctum sanctorum, in which was placed a bundle of Burmese tracts, with a copy of St. Matthew's Gospel. One of their number had taken the office of teacher upon himself—cut his hair short, wore a close cap decorated with rows of the golden-green wing-cases of buprestis beetles, and dressed himself in a long white robe like a Mahomedan imaum. On their worship days the teacher, or some other of their number who could read Burmese, read a portion of Matthew or one of the tracts, and they were then laid in the little temple, when all prostrated themselves and worshipped the books. The teacher prayed before us most eloquently for the spread of Christianity, and readily agreed, as did his people, to purge the chapel of everything objectionable, and render his worship more like the teaching of the scriptures. Next rainy season this teacher called on me in

Tavoy, professing himself a sincere believer; but he said, when he began to require the people to act in accordance with the Scriptures, they drove him out of the settlement. They were all ready to worship the Bible, prostrating themselves and knocking their heads on the ground, but not one was willing to obey the precepts it enjoined."

At Tavoy I was present at an examination of a Karen school, which was under the training of the Rev. Mr. Cross, a most indefatigable labourer. The youths, who were quiet in demeanour and intelligent-looking, were questioned on scripture history, the principles of the Christian religion, elementary science, and arithmetic by the deputy-commissioner, the doctor, and other visitors, as well as by Mr. Cross himself. They answered readily and for the most part correctly, appearing fully to understand and enter into the several subjects.

CHAPTER XXII.

Burman War of 1824–6—Causes which led to it—The Andaman Islands and their Inhabitants—The British land and take possession of Rangoon—Actions at Yang-hoo and Joazoang—Defeat of the Burmans.

In a work that relates chiefly to the Tenasserim provinces, it may not be out of place to present a brief sketch of the war by which they became an integral part of the British Empire. I shall endeavour to do this in the following pages, but for a fuller account I must refer the reader to the works of Colonel Symes, Major Snodgrass, and a few others, who have been my principal authorities.

The Peguans and other neighbouring nations having been conquered by the victorious arms of the Burmans, and absorbed into their empire, they not unnaturally fell into the error of supposing that no power could stand against them, and the conquest of Bengal, as well as the other British possessions in Hindoostan, became the object of their ambition. The king lent a willing ear to the flatteries of his officers, particularly his great general Maha Bandoola (a title signifying one who moves with the agility of a monkey). "Wherefore," said he, "should we not take the provinces of the English?" "Give me but an army, and I will conquer the whole country." He was at last gratified by leading troops through the Aeng pass to attack our eastern frontier, which was then by no means in an efficient state of defence; and it is even said he took with him a pair of golden fetters wherewith to bind the Governor-General, who was to be dragged a prisoner to the golden footstool. The British landing meanwhile at Rangoon, he was quickly recalled in order to defend his country from the very people he had gone to attack.

A belief also obtained amongst the Burmans that their king was one day to rule over the British territories westward of the Ganges. They had formed a very erroneous opinion not only of the Sepoys, but also of the British troops; and it was in utter ignorance of the enemy with whom they had to deal, and with blind infatuation as to consequences, that they provoked a power before which Tippo and the fierce Mahrattas had succumbed. "To kill and crush the rebel strangers—to let none escape, but, by dint of his golden majesty's omnipotence—to destroy and utterly annihilate the wild foreigners," were the orders issued by the king; and such-like feats the generals thought themselves sure of accomplishing.

Numerous acts of aggression and provocation had been committed by the Burmans against the Anglo-Indian government, arising chiefly out of the emigration of the Arracanese into the territories of the East India Company, from whence they made hostile incursions into the Burman dominions, and then again sought the protection of the British flag. But towards the end of the year 1823 an outrage was committed by the Burmans, which, as all reparation and apology was refused, left no alternative but a declaration of war. This was an attack on Suparee, a little sterile island or sandbank situated at the mouth of the Nauf, a river of Chittagong. Of this the Burmans took possession, expelling the few Sepoys who had been stationed there. No time was lost in re-capturing the island; but to all remonstrances and representations the Burman government turned a deaf ear, plainly enough showing that the king sanctioned, if he did not instigate, the lawless proceedings of his generals. Our eastern frontier, which indeed possessed but a few scattered regiments of Sepoys for its defence, was exposed to the predatory incursions of marauding parties from Assam and Munipore. Early in 1824 frequent skirmishes took place between the Company's troops and the invaders, in which the latter were always discomfited. On the 21st of February, however, a disaster happened which rendered it imperative to act with decision and no longer to trifle with the danger that threatened our Indian possessions. Lieut.-Colonel Bowen, with a force of fifteen hundred Sepoys, attacked a party of Burmans two thousand strong, who had taken up a position at Doodputlee, which they had strengthened according to custom by a stockade. He met on this occasion with a serious check, losing five officers and one hundred and fifty men. After this repulse only one course was open to the British authorities, and a formal declaration of war was the result. It was determined that Rangoon should be taken possession of, as being the principal sea-port of the Burman empire, and affording easy access into the interior of the country by means of the Irrawaddy; and it was hoped that submission and reparation would be made as soon as the town should be taken by the invading army. A force of from five thousand to six thousand men was speedily organised and placed under the command of Brigadier-General Sir Archibald Campbell; and the land-locked harbour of Port Cornwallis, in the Great Andaman Island, was the appointed place of rendezvous. These solitary isles have a beautiful appearance as they first break upon the sight of those approaching from the Indian coast, especially after the flat country around Calcutta. The mountains, which are covered with luxuriant vegetation down to the water's edge, rise green and beautiful out of the white surf that dashes at their base, and, crowned by the sombre "Saddle Peak," tower to a considerable height. Beautiful shells—gorgonias, madrepores, and cowries—lie thick upon the shore. The romantic scenery, the teeming luxuriance of the vegetable world, contrasts strangely with the stunted growth and ugly features of the wretched savages who inhabit these island solitudes. Their dwellings are the rudest, and their only clothing the thick mud with which they plaster themselves as a protection against the swarms of insects that attack their otherwise naked bodies. They subsist chiefly on shell-fish, which are very abundant, but they are sometimes, in inclement weather, reduced to the greatest straits. Their only weapons are the bow, arrow, and dart. In the dense forests, which occupy so large a portion of these isles, grow the spreading banyan, the almond-tree, the giant iron-tree whose tough grain turns back the edge of the sharpest axe, the red-tree which rivals mahogany in the beauty of its wood, the cocoa-nut palm, whilst around their trunks entwine innumerable creepers, forming an impenetrable barrier. A settlement was established by the East India Company, in the year 1791, in the southern part of the Great Andaman; but in 1793 it was removed, by the advice of Admiral Cornwallis, to the spot that now bears his name. It was designed for a convict establishment and as a shelter for ships during the north-east monsoon; but the unhealthiness of the climate compelled its entire abandonment in the year 1796.

In November last (1857) the Hon. Company's steamer Pluto left Maulmain for the Andamans, for the purpose of conveying thither several scientific gentlemen deputed by Government to report upon these islands, with a view to again establish a settlement in some favourable locality; a measure of great importance in many points of view. The expedition was accompanied by several experienced photographers, so that scenes which civilized man has never beheld, and on which the artist has never tried his skill, will be copied with a fidelity that no pencil can imitate, and rendered familiar to the world.

But to return to the year 1824. By the 4th of May the ships Liffey, Larne, Sophie, and Slaney, belonging to the Royal Navy, forty transports, and several Company's cruisers, having on board the 41st Regiment, a Madras European regiment, and six regiments of Sepoys, reached Port Cornwallis; these troops, with others which were to follow, making a force of nearly ten thousand men. The fleet left the harbour and stood to sea on the morning of the 5th, and after a fine run anchored off the mouth of the Rangoon river. The Burmans were taken quite by surprise. The alarm was quickly given by means of beacons at the guard-houses at the entrance of the river, and at night blazing fires signalled the danger that threatened the dominions of "the Lord of Earth and Air;" whilst the people could be discerned flying into the interior with bundles on their heads containing the most valuable of their worldly possessions.

On the 11th the ships advanced up the river, the Liffey leading the van, and the same evening they reached Rangoon and anchored at the King's wharf. The consternation of the authorities was great; and their first thought was to revenge themselves on the Europeans living in Rangoon. Accordingly, the British merchants and the American missionaries (between whom the Burmans could not make any distinction) were seized, fettered, and locked up in the Custom House, whence they were dragged to the Hall of Justice, bullied, threatened, and driven again to prison. They were finally condemned to die, and their inhuman jailors made every preparation for their execution, sharpening and exhibiting before them the instruments of death; but the authorities, dreading probably the vengeance of the invading force, delayed from time to time to carry out the sentence, and at last a shot from the Liffey put a sudden stop to their deliberations, and compelled them to seek safety in flight. The prisoners were sent up the country, and after enduring great hardships were in the end rescued.

And now commenced that defensive system of warfare which the Burmans always adopt in presence of a superior enemy. The government assembled the whole of the inhabitants of Rangoon, and, placing them under the command of officers and slaves of the government, had them driven like cattle into the jungles, leaving behind a deserted city which could afford no support or assistance to the invading army; and so perished the hopes long entertained that the inhabitants would accept the protection of the British (promises of which had been circulated amongst the people), and afford them the means of transport by boats up the Irrawaddy. The British force landed and took possession of the deserted town. Proclamations were despatched by stragglers, inviting them to return and accept protection, but in vain, for their wives and children, who were held as hostages by the Burman chiefs, would in that case have been put to death. Meanwhile, the tocsin of war sounding throughout the country, called the people to arms, and a strong force was organised with all the haste of which the Burman government was capable. War-boats covered the Irrawaddy, and every preparation was made for driving the foreigners into the sea from whence they came. The south-west monsoon now brought about the rainy season in this part of the country, and the jungles swarmed with armed men skilled in desultory warfare.

The first action of any consequence took place on the 28th of May, when Sir A. Campbell decided on making a reconnoissance, and for this purpose advanced from the lines with a force composed of two companies of the 13th Light Infantry, one hundred strong; the flank companies of the 38th Regiment, two hundred; four hundred Native Infantry, and two field-pieces. The latter had, however, to be left behind in consequence of the state of the ground, which was saturated by the pouring rain, and knee-deep in mud.

It was found that the enemy had taken up a strong position at the villages of Yanghoo and Joazoang, flanked by a jungle, and defended by two stockades, from which a heavy fire was opened on the advancing troops, who were unable to reply by a single shot; their muskets having been rendered quite useless by the rain. The Burmans received the attacking force with a terrific yell, the beating of tomtoms, and loud cries of "Come, come!" They made a gallant defence, exhibited a remarkable contempt of death, and neither gave nor expected quarter. The stockades, which were garrisoned by about fifteen hundred men (the whole force numbering some seven thousand), were quickly stormed. three or four hundred of the enemy losing their lives in the defence.

"The stockades of Joazoang," says an eye-witness, "were of an irregular shape; the parapet was about four feet high, made of piles driven into the ground, and banked up by earth taken from a trench in the interior of about three feet deep, so that a person standing in the trench was completely under cover from the fire of the assailants. In the face of the stockade large bamboos were fixed, which answered as loopholes through which to fire, and large mats were strongly fastened on the outside of the parapet, so as to prevent the interior being seen, and also to preclude the possibility of getting over the scaling ladders. But the most material defence of a stockade was in the abattis by which it was surrounded. This is made with branches of trees pointed at the end, and firmly and thickly planted in the ground; they are succeeded by rows of sharp bamboo-spikes, which, in the heat of the moment, being unobserved, penetrate deep into the feet, and occasion wounds of the most painful nature; the whole is surrounded by two rows of railing, so that, if a good fire is kept up from the work itself, the obstacles to be surmounted are far from despicable."

After burning these stockades, as night was drawing on, the troops returned to quarter, having given the Burmans a salutary lesson as to the sort of enemy with whom they had to deal.

CHAPTER XXIII.

The Burmans pretend to negotiate—Advance of the British on Kemmendine, and Storming of the Advanced Works—Kemmendine taken possession of—Sickness in the British Camp—Storming of Kummeroot—Expedition against Tavoy and Mergui—The Princes of Tongho and Sarrawaddy join the Burman Army—Syriam captured—Attack of the "Invulnerables" on the Pagoda—Scarcity of fresh Provisions—Descent upon Martaban and Yeh—A Detachment advances to Pegu.

After the affair of Joazoang, the Burmans commenced stockading the heights of Kemmendine (a village three miles above Rangoon), and rendering them as impregnable as possible; but, fearing an attack whilst these works were in progress, they made a pretence of negotiating, and accordingly, on the 9th of June two war-boats, each containing fifty men, and bearing a flag of truce, arrived at Rangoon. Two deputies, one the ex-governor of Bassein, desired a conference with the English general, which was readily granted. The ex-governor inquired "Why the English had come with soldiers and ships, and what they wanted?" The reasons were fully explained, and, after many evasive replies, they requested a truce of a few days, in order to consult an officer of rank at some distance; but, as their object was plainly to gain time, their proposition was negatived.

At two o'clock the following morning three thousand men moved forward to attack Kemmendine, taking with them four eighteen-pounders, besides field-pieces and heavy mortars, all of which had to be dragged through the mud by the men, as no draught animals could be procured.

The road to Kemmendine runs parallel to the river, and at about a mile and a half from Rangoon takes its course over a hill of moderate elevation. Here was planted a stockade, which it was necessary to capture before any further advances could be made. This was quickly done, and no time was lost in hastening onward to the Great Kemmendine stockade, which was partly concealed from view by the dense jungle surrounding it. When reached it was too late to commence the attack that day, and the troops had to pass the night without even the protection of great coats, and exposed to a deluge of rain, which poured down incessantly.

"The night we passed in this situation," remarks one who experienced the hardships he describes, "was such as may easily be imagined. Soft mud for the bed of such as choose to lie down, and the trunk of a tree for a pillow; but so powerful an anodyne is fatigue, that, notwithstanding these disadvantages, accompanied by continual firing and the yells of the enemy, many slept soundly, or passed the night joyfully anticipating the approaching attack on the enemy.

"The shouts of the Burmans had a curious effect, heightened by the wild scenery of the dark gloomy forest which surrounded us. First, a low murmur might be heard, rising as it were gradually in tone, and followed by the wild and loud huzza of thousands of voices; then again all was silence, save now and then a straggling shot or challenge from our sentries; and soon after another peal of voices would resound through the trees. This they continued all night, but towards morning the yells became fainter and fainter, and at daybreak they totally ceased."

At this time a more insidious foe entered the British camp, and struck down many a stalwart frame. Disease, brought on by exposure to the weather, the soldiers on guard being often up to their knees in mud, sent many to their graves, and a still greater number to the hospital, from which indeed there was little chance of returning, for salt beef and biscuit were alone obtainable as food, and, on such diet, those once attacked with dysentery could have small prospect of recovering. The whole country, for miles around, had been swept of cattle and food of every description, and even evacuated by the inhabitants, in accordance with the policy adopted by the Burman government.

On the 1st of July some skirmishing took place, in which the Sykia Woon-gyee and his men were completely defeated, and forced to retreat.

A new commander, the Shumbah Woon-gyee, was appointed, who lost no time in throwing up a number of formidable stockades in a position of great strength at Pagoda Point, about seven miles from Rangoon, and also at Kummeroot, where the main army was entrenched. Sir A. Campbell determined to dislodge this force, and capture the stockades without delay. Brigadier-General Macbean had the command of the land troops, which were composed of one thousand British soldiers and five hundred Sepoys, while the Commander-in-Chief, with another column of considerable strength, and attended by gun-boats, proceeded by water. Arrived on the field of action, a heavy cannonade was opened on the stockade, which soon silenced the enemy's guns. The storming party, made up of detachments from the King's 41st regiment, and the 17th Madras

Native Infantry, commanded by Lieut.-Col. Godwin and Major Wahab, effected a landing, and in a very short space of time captured the great stockade. The attack of the land-column was equally spirited. Brigadier-General M'Creagh, with five hundred men from the 13th and 38th regiments, commanded by Majors Sale and Frith, advanced to the attack.

The first stockade was captured in a few moments, and then the troops rushed on stockade after stockade, until the works were carried in every direction. The enemy had taken refuge in an inner stockade, into which a party entered and drove them out on the bayonets of their comrades. "The panic that now took place among the Burmans," says the authority before quoted, "can scarcely be described; rushing in crowds towards the only gate through which they might escape, they completely choked it up; others then attempted to climb over the walls, but were mowed down by our shot, and those at the gate were falling by dozens.

Some became quite desperate, and with their long dishevelled hair streaming over their shoulders, and giving them the most ferocious appearance, seized their swords with both hands, and dashed on the bayonets of the soldiers, where they met that death which they seemed alternately to fear and despise; whilst others hid themselves in the trenches full of water, and there lay motionless, feigning to be dead. The carnage was very great, at least five hundred men being slain in the main stockade, and amongst them was the Shumbah Woon-gyee. When the firing first commenced he had been wounded, and his attendants were carrying him into the jungles amidst a host of fugitives, when he received another shot, which terminated his existence. Many other chieftains of rank also fell: one had attacked a soldier of the Thirteenth, and was in the act of cutting him down, when Major Sale came to his assistance, and, having felled the Burman to the ground, rescued the soldier from his perilous situation." These works, which were of great extent, embracing ten stockades, and well mounted with artillery, had been defended by ten or twelve thousand men, one thousand of whom, it was estimated, were killed; while the loss on the side of the British did not amount to more than about fifty men. This success had the effect of dispersing for a time the Burman army.

The rain continued without intermission, and the sickness amongst the European troops rapidly increased. As no advance could be made before the month of January, the intermediate time was improved by fitting out an expedition for the capture of the maritime possessions of the Burman monarch. It comprised the 89th King's Regiment and the 7th Madras Native Infantry, under the command of Lieut.-Col. Mills. The object in view was speedily accomplished. Tavoy surrendered, Mergui was captured, and the whole of the Tenasserim provinces accepted British protection.

The Princes of Tongho and Sarrawaddy, brothers of the King, arrived at the seat of war about this time, with the intention of directing in person the operations of the Burman army, aided by certain astrologers, in whom this people place great faith; nor was this all, the King's "Invulnerables" were likewise despatched from Ava, to effect by supernatural agency what had hitherto been attempted in vain by ordinary soldiers. These fanatics are regarded by their countrymen as quite proof against the assaults of all enemies whatsoever. Mystic signs, as well as representations of the most ferocious animals, are tatooed upon their skin, and charms, consisting of small pieces of gold, silver, and precious stones, bearing cabalistic characters, are inserted in their bodies. They generally expose themselves with the utmost recklessness to the fire of an enemy, dancing a war-dance in the most dangerous part of the works, and shouting defiance to those who are audacious enough to contend with so terrible a foe.

The old fort of Syriam was next taken from a detachment of Burmans holding possession of it, and the stockades on the Dalla river were destroyed.

At last the night of the 30th of August was declared by the astrologers in the Burman camp to be a lucky time for attacking the British lines, and accordingly the "Invulnerables" rushed to the attack, armed with swords and muskets, muttering incantations, and yelling in the most frightful manner; their determination was to retake the Great Dagon Pagoda of Rangoon, and celebrate their annual festival. They were met by a detachment of the 38th Regiment, and at the same time a few rounds of grape were poured into their crowded ranks from the British ramparts. They stood but a moment before the storm, and then flying for their lives sought refuge in the neighbouring jungle.

During the months of September and October the hospitals continued thickly tenanted, and fresh provisions were extremely scarce. A few buffaloes were sometimes brought in, but they were reserved for the sick. What little food, of the description so much needed, could be procured from the ships, sold at an extravagant price. Fowls and ducks for eight rupees each; geese, sixteen rupees; sheep, worth two rupees at Calcutta, fetched thirty rupees on the shores of the Irrawaddy; whilst a cow and a calf, at an auction on board one of the ships, were knocked down at three hundred rupees.

Numerous actions took place in capturing stockades on the Dalla, Palang, and Lyne rivers. At Kykloo the troops met with a repulse, owing to an unwonted panic seizing the Sepoys.

It was now determined to make a descent upon Martaban, the only remaining town of any consequence on the coast of which the invaders had not gained possession. Martaban lies about one hundred miles to the east of Rangoon, on the left bank of the Salween river, and four miles above what is now the flourishing town of Maulmain, the capital of the Tenasserim provinces, and which is situated on the opposite side of the river. A detachment, consisting of part of the 41st Regiment and three hundred men of the 3rd Madras Native Infantry, sailed from Rangoon on the 12th October for the capture of Martaban. The ship missed the entrance of the river, and in consequence did not reach its destination as soon as was expected; but finally the object of the expedition was accomplished in gallant style. The town was bombarded, and then taken by assault, with the loss of not much more than thirty men.

A force was also sent from Rangoon to the town of Pegu, under the command of Lieut.-Colonel Mallet, of the 98th Regiment. It left the former place on the 27th of November, and caused the greatest terror to the inhabitants of the country through which it passed. One of the party relates the following:—"Whilst," he says, "we were walking about the vicinity of a village, we discovered, in a remote spot, under the shade of a clump of bamboos, a poor man and his family, who were crouching under the bushes in the greatest terror. It is impossible to figure an unfortunate being more under the influence of fear than he was. He threw himself at our feet, and repeatedly lifting his hands to his head begged for life, not doubting but that it was our intention to put an end to his existence; with much difficulty he was persuaded to the contrary, and informed that he would be remunerated for anything taken from the village; and, his fears being at last calmed, he went back and shortly returned with his family, consisting of his aged mother, his wife, who was an interesting-looking young woman, and two children. When they had been placed in possession of their former habitation, the man recovered his composure, and the old lady, who had been staring about with the imbecility of extreme old age, began to recognise objects familiar to her, and immediately commenced collecting her household utensils, which had been scattered around. The young woman could not be so easily quieted, but exhibited the deepest despair; untying her hair she shook it wildly over her shoulders, and striking her breast, and knocking her forehead against the ground, she pleaded for mercy, which we never thought of withholding. The terror caused by our sudden appearance is not to be wondered at, as we had hitherto held no communication with the surrounding villages; and the natives, merely hearing of the white strangers through the medium of exaggerated reports, no doubt considered us to be ferocious and sanguinary to the greatest degree."

This detachment left Pegu on the evening of the 30th instant and returned to Rangoon, having encountered no opposition during its absence.

CHAPTER XXIV.

Advance of Maha Bandoola and his Army—Actions before Rangoon—Fire-rafts—The Maha Bandoola retires with his Army and takes up his position at Kokeen—Storming of the Works by the British Troops—The Burman Army driven from their Fortifications—The Maha Bandoola reorganises his Army at Donoobew.

MEANWHILE more formidable foes than the invading army had yet encountered were wending their way, under the command of the celebrated Maha Bandoola, across the mountains and through the pestiferous jungles of Arracan. This great general had to conduct his troops a distance of upwards of two hundred miles at the most inclement season of the year; a march which no European troops, under such circumstances, could have accomplished; but the Burman soldier, with chopper in hand and a bag of rice containing food for a fortnight, moves forward undeterred by difficulties from which troops that far surpass him in actual warfare would shrink. This army, numbered at sixty thousand fighting men, composed of the flower of the Burman troops, was made up of elements as novel to the British soldier as they were wild and picturesque. There were Cassay horsemen mounted on steeds richly caparisoned, and armed with swords and spears. The musketeers numbered thirty-five thousand men. The "Invulnerables," trusting in charms and spells, and drunk with opium, excited the fanaticism of their fellow-soldiers by a continued display of their own. There were also those who carried implements for stockading and entrenching; in short, it was as efficient an army as the King of Ava could possibly send into the field. The general rendezvous was at Donoobew, to which place recruits were hastening from all parts of the kingdom to join the grand army.

Every preparation was made by the British general to receive this formidable array. The great pagoda was well garrisoned and strongly fortified; numerous pieces of artillery being mounted on its terraces. Three hundred men of the 38th Regiment occupied the interior, and at its base was stationed the 28th Madras Native Infantry. The 13th Light Infantry occupied the heights between the pagoda and the town; while the remainder of the army took up a position adjacent to the stockade at Rangoon. Kemmendine was garrisoned by the 26th Madras Native Infantry. On the 1st of December a series of actions commenced in front of Rangoon. Kemmendine was attacked, but in their attempts on this post the enemy was completely foiled. Dense columns issued from the forest, forming a line extending from the jungle near the pagoda to within gun-shot distance of Rangoon. Laying aside their arms, they commenced intrenching, throwing up a parapet of earth, behind which they found shelter from the opposing army. "The moving masses," remarks Major Snodgrass, "which had so lately attracted our anxious attention, had sunk into the ground, and to any one who had not witnessed the whole scene, the existence of these subterranean legions would not have been credited. The occasional movement of a chief, with his gilt chattah (umbrella), from place to place, superintending the progress of their labour, was the only thing that now attracted notice. By a distant observer, the hills covered with mounds would have been taken for anything rather than the approaches of an attacking army; but to us, who had watched the whole proceeding, it seemed the work of magic or enchantment."

Sir A. Campbell, considering it desirable to drive them from these works, directed Major Sale, with the 13th Light Infantry and the 18th Madras Native Infantry, commanded by Captain Ross, to execute the movement, which was effected in gallant style, by forcing the entrenchments and taking the advancing force in flank, but not without severe loss. Captain O'Shea was killed and several other officers wounded. These trenches, which are so characteristic of the Burman plan of warfare, are thus described by the officer quoted above: "They were found to be a succession of holes, capable of containing two men each, and excavated, so as to afford shelter both from the weather and the fire of the enemy; even a shell lighting in the trench could at most but kill two men. As it is not the Burman system to relieve their troops in making these approaches, each hole contained a sufficient supply of rice, water, and even fuel, for its inmates; and under the excavated bank a bed of straw or brushwood was prepared, in which one man could sleep while his comrade watched. When one line of trenches is completed, its occupiers, taking advantage of the night, push forward to where the second line is to be opened, their place being immediately taken up by fresh troops from the rear, and so on progressively, the number of trenches occupied varying according to the force of the besiegers, to the plans of the general, or the nature of the ground." Towards the close of the day the occupation of the trenches was resumed by the Burmans, and again attacking Kemmendine they were a second time repulsed. Indefatigable attempts were made to destroy the British shipping by fire-rafts, and it was only by constant attention, and the use of grappling-irons, that the wooden walls were saved from destruction. These rafts, which are sometimes one hundred feet in length, were formed of bamboos, so arranged by means of hinges, and other contrivances, that no sooner does one come in contact with a vessel, or any obstacle, than it separates and surrounds it with flaming materials, such as dried wood, petroleum, cotton, and other combustibles.

The Burmans always took advantage of the night to strengthen their position. On the 5th instant the left wing of their army, being favourably situated for attack, it was determined, if possible, to deal a blow that would lessen their power. Accordingly, whilst Chads, of the Royal Navy, was directed to proceed up the river, to the rear of the hostile force, two columns attacked their entrenchments. One of these, eight hundred or a thousand strong, under Major Sale, stormed the centre of the enemy's lines, while the other, six hundred strong, under Major Walker, took the Burmans in flank. The column under Major Walker was first engaged, making a dashing assult on the lines. It was received, however, with a well-directed fire, and its brave commander lost his life while leading on his men. The trenches were speedily carried, and their defenders swept away at the bayonet's point. Major Sale's detachment forced the centre of the wing, the whole of which was now broken, and the two columns, having effected a junction, pursued the fugitives, about six thousand in number, and completely cleared the works, leaving behind only the dead and wounded. Subsequent attacks were made, in which the Burmans were invariably defeated, and on the 8th instant the vast multitude, and their redoubtable leader, who had advanced with such terrible threats, fell back to Kokeen, four miles from the Great Pagoda; here Bandoola rallied his scattered forces, and in a short space of time threw up extensive fortifications.

The British army was at this time beset with more dangerous foes than those who met them in the field of battle. Incendiaries, the emissaries of the Burman government, were lurking in Rangoon (built, like all Burman towns, of the most inflammable materials) to burn out the army which by force of arms they were unable to dislodge. On one occasion half the town was destroyed before the flames could be got under, but this was at last accomplished by the united efforts of the troops. On the 15th instant preparations were made for attacking the fresh position taken up by Bandoola and his troops at Kokeen. The works were three miles in circumference, and of the most formidable description. Two strongly-built stockades were connected by six circular entrenchments, and defended by an abattis.

The columns of attack consisted of the 13th Light Infantry and the 18th Madras Infantry, commanded by Brigadier-General Cotton. The 38th, 41st, and 89th British regiments, with some detachments of native infantry, were led on by Sir A. Campbell in person. In about twenty minutes they had driven the Burmans from the ramparts, and gained entire possession of the fortifications, dispersing a force amounting to twenty-five thousand men, with a loss to themselves of sixteen officers and one hundred and forty men killed and wounded. The loss on the side of the Burmans from the 1st to the 15th instant was estimated at six thousand men, and that of the invading army, during the same period, amounted to forty officers and five hundred men killed and wounded. The Commander-in-Chief fully appreciated the bravery of his men, of whom, on this occasion, he wrote as follows:

"When it is known that thirteen hundred British infantry stormed and carried by assault the most formidably entrenched works

I ever saw, defended by upwards of twenty thousand men, I trust it is unnecessary for me to say more in praise of soldiers performing such a prodigy; future ages will scarcely believe it."

This decisive action terminated the operations before Rangoon. Bandoola retired with so much of his army as he could hold together to Donoobew, where he commenced re-organising his forces. The victorious troops returned the same evening to cantonments.

CHAPTER XXV.

The Inhabitants of Rangoon return to the city—Arrival of fresh Troops—The British Forces march on Donoobew—Repulse of General Cotton—The British Columns effect a junction—Prepare to storm Donoobew—Death of Maha Bandoola and Evacuation of Donoobew by the Burman Army, 2nd of April—The March resumed April 4th—Pretended Negotiation—Evacuation of Prome—Which city the British enter 25th of April—Opinions entertained by the Burmans of the British Soldiers—The Army enters into Winter Quarters.

THE retreat of the Burman army permitted the peaceably-disposed inhabitants of Rangoon to return to their native city, which they did in considerable numbers, after experiencing the greatest hardships and privations in the jungles. In a short time a bazaar was opened, from which fruit and vegetables, venison and fish were procurable. The British forces were likewise reinforced by the arrival of fresh troops, comprising the first troop of the Bengal Horse Artillery, the Rocket Troop, some squadrons of cavalry, the 47th Regiment, and also several battalions of Madras native infantry.

It was now determined to penetrate into the interior of the country as the only means of making a lasting impression on the Burman government, and on the 11th of February the land-column, commanded by Sir A. Campbell, began its march from Rangoon. Numerically it was not much more than two thousand strong. There were thirteen hundred European infantry, one thousand Sepoys, a troop of Horse Artillery, and a rocket troop. This force was to march up the left bank of the Irrawaddy, and to join the water-column in the neighbourhood of Donoobew. This latter was composed of eight hundred European infantry, a battalion of Sepoys, with a train of Artillery, and commanded by Brigadier-General Cotton. It embarked in a flotilla of sixty boats (carrying artillery), which was under the command of Captain Alexander,

R.N. The boats of the men-of-war lying at Rangoon, together with upwards of one hundred British seamen, accompanied the expedition, which was to sail up the Palang river into the Irrawaddy and push on to Donoobew with all possible expedition. General Cotton arrived there with his detachment on the 4th of March, and immediately summoned Maha Bandoola to surrender, when, on receiving a refusal, he determined on making an attack without waiting for the land-column. Accordingly on the 7th he commenced the assault, and succeeded in carrying the pagoda stockade, with a loss to the enemy of four hundred men in killed and wounded. The detachment, however, under Captain Rose, which had been ordered to storm the second work, met with a repulse, Captains Rose and Cannon, with several men, perishing in the attempt. On this General Cotton, finding the works of greater strength than he had anticipated, withdrew his forces, after having lost five officers and one hundred and thirty men.

The fortifications of Donoobew were defended by a Burman army of fifteen thousand men, with one hundred and fifty pieces of cannon, and three hundred jingals. News of this disaster being conveyed to the land-column, it at once crossed the Irrawaddy on rafts—a work of much difficulty and danger, but which, by indefatigable exertions, was accomplished in five days, and on the 25th of March it arrived in front of Donoobew. The stockade at this place was of great strength, composed of solid beams of teak, and defended by a formidable battery. The ramparts bristled with bayonets and spears, whilst here and there the gilt chattahs of the chiefs glittered in the sun. After several sorties, which were repelled without much loss on either side, the detachment having effected a junction, a general assault was planned for the 2nd of April; and on the morning of that day the thunder of the English battery announced that the decisive moment had arrived. There was, however, no reply from the Burman fort, and the unexpected intelligence was conveyed to the

British camp that the general Maha Bandoola was dead—having been killed the previous day by the fragment of a shell while inspecting the defences; and dismay, in consequence, seizing his troops, they had only awaited for the approach of night to evacuate the place with all speed.

One man, who was found in the fort with both his feet shot off, gave the following account of the death of his chief, as reported by Major Snodgrass:—"I belong to the household of Maha Bandoola, and my business was to beat the great drums that are hanging in the verandah of the woon-gyee's house. Yesterday morning, between the hours of nine and ten, while the chief's dinner was preparing, he went out to take his usual morning walk round the works, and arrived at his observatory (that tower with a red ball upon it), where, as there was no firing, he sat down upon a couch that was kept there for his use. While he was giving orders the English began throwing bombs, and one of them, falling close to the woon-gyee, burst and killed him on the spot. His body was immediately carried away and burned to ashes. His death was soon known to everybody in the stockade, and the soldiers refused to stay and fight under any other commander. The chiefs lost all influence and command over their men, every individual thinking only of providing for his own personal safety."

Maha Bandoola had been the leader of the war faction, and was by his courage and strength of character eminently calculated to command such troops as composed the Burman army. As an instance of his discipline, an officer relates the following:—"When we entered Donoobew, a basket," he says, "containing the head of a man was found tied to one of the guns in the water-battery. This was said to have appertained to one of their artillerymen, who, having seen all the men at a gun killed or wounded by one of our discharges, had shown great unwillingness to supply their place, which the Bandoola observing, he instantly ordered his head to be struck off. This example had the desired effect, and the gun was again manned."

With this general perished the main hope of the Burman court. "The account of this event," says the same authority, "was transmitted to the king in a letter from the Prince of Sarawaddy, who, commencing with a long preamble about the extraordinary effect of the English artillery, the king flew into a violent rage, and said, 'What! can my brother find nothing to write about but praises of the rebel strangers?' On continuing the perusal he found it contained the intimation of the Bandoola's death and fall of Donoobew, and the news so much affected him that he shut himself up in his palace, and would not communicate with any one for many days."

In the place which had been so hastily evacuated was found a vast quantity of ammunition; even the prisoners had in the hurry been left behind.

The invading force now pushed on to Prome, which was being fortified with all possible expedition by the army which had fled from Donoobew. On the 4th of April the march recommenced. The way was through a desolate country, marked here and there by smoking villages; for the policy of the Burmans was to leave behind them a desert without either inhabitants or supplies of any kind. In one part, however, the troops for three miles marched under the leafy screen of a grove of mango trees, the cool shade proving a great boon to the way-worn and weary soldiers. On the 19th inst. the Burman chief in command at Prome intimated a desire to negotiate; but, as he at the same time requested Sir A. Campbell to stay his advance, it became evident that the only object in view was to gain time for completing the defences of the city. The proposal was therefore negatived, though the English General expressed his readiness to listen to proposals made with a sincere desire for peace. On the 25th instant the British army reached Prome, from which place, as in the instance of Donoobew, the Burmans made a hasty retreat, the rapid advance of the columns not allowing them time to complete their plan of defence. But had the pretended negotiations been listened to, and a halt permitted, many valuable lives must have been sacrificed in storming the place. The retreating Burmans had, however, fired the town in several places; but by great exertions the flames were got under, and finally extinguished.

One hundred pieces of cannon were found mounted on the walls, and in the arsenal a plentiful supply of powder and military stores, while the magazine contained a sufficient quantity of rice to furnish the army with food for a year. After possession had been taken of the city the civil magistrate returned, and was reinstated in his office by the British authorities. The inhabitants of Prome, likewise, and the neighbouring towns took courage and resumed their peaceable occupations. The king now made great exertions to recruit his forces, and pecuniary inducements were held out to all who would join the royal army. One hundred and fifty ticals, or nearly 20*l.*, were offered to recruits, a thing never before known. An event which still further alarmed the Burman government, was the conquest of Arracan by Brigadier-General Morison.

The erroneous opinion which had been formed of the British soldiers by the Burmans at the commencement of the war had by this time undergone a great change. "Previous to the war," says Mr. Judson, "they had a better opinion of them than of the Hindoos, but considered them luxurious and effeminate, incapable of standing the fatigues of war, and therefore unable to contend with a people hardy like themselves, who carry on war with but little food and no shelter.

"They now consider them nearly invincible, fierce, and blood-thirsty, and discovering almost supernatural prowess. I have heard them compare them in action to a particular class of demons called Balu, that, according to Burman notions, feed on human flesh. They have compared the rapidity of their movements to a whirlwind. The skill of the Europeans in the use of artillery, and especially in that of rockets and shells, astonishes them, and is incomprehensible to them. I should add, that the forbearance and moderation of the European troops after victory, and their obedience to command and regularity of discipline, is a subject of admiration with them. In comparison with the Sepoys, they also observe, that they are indifferent to plunder.

"The first circumstance of the war which made a deep impression on the Burman court was the sudden and complete destruction, to use the language of the Burmans themselves, of the Thongba-Woon-gyee and of his party of about one thousand men, in a stockade near Rangoon. I heard from a Burman who was present in the action, and who for some political offence, on his return to Ava, became my fellow-prisoner, that this was effected by about three hundred Europeans. The court, being displeased with the procrastination of Ki-Woon-gyee, had sent Thongba-Woon-gyee to supersede him. This person was determined to fight. He sent, I think, an Armenian as a spy to Rangoon, who brought back news that the English were preparing to attack his stockade. The messenger was put to death for bringing accounts tending to discourage the troops; but the execution was hardly over when the troops presented themselves before the stockade.

"My informant and other persons afterwards gave a most appalling account of the attack of the 'Balus,' as they called them. The gate of the stockade was choked up by the runaways, and almost every man in it put to death by the bayonet. Thongba-Woon-gyee was killed in the fight by one of his own people. This mode of attack was totally contrary to all that the Burmans knew of war, and struck them with consternation. They stated that when one of the assailants was killed another immediately took his place, and that they were not to be discouraged from advancing even when wounded; so that it was in vain to contend with such an enemy. Their imaginations were so wrought upon, that to these particulars they added many fabulous ones, such as that the Europeans continued to advance after their hands had been chopped off in scrambling over the stockades; that the arms and legs of the wounded were carefully picked up and replaced by the English surgeons, who were represented as skilful as the warriors were bold.

"The next circumstance which brought about the revolution in question, was the defeat of Bandoola in his lines before Rangoon, and his flight to Donoobew—an event which struck the Burmans dumb, and for a time made them consider their affairs desperate. They thought the British army would then immediately march upon Ava. The princesses of Pugan and Shwa-dong, with the queen-mother, when the news arrived in Ava, sent for Mrs. Judson, and communicated to her the particulars of Bandoola's defeat. The princess of Pugan said on that occasion, 'The Bandoola's troops have piled up their arms for the use of the foreigners; they have all dispersed, and the enemy has nothing to do but to march to Ava clapping their hands.' Mrs. Judson's advice was asked by the princesses. They wished to know whether they ought to run away or stay; whether there was any chance of safety for them. They entreated her protection and good offices with the English. Upon the failure at Donoobew the Burmans again somewhat recovered their spirits, and Bandoola was supported by all the strength the country could afford. The death of Bandoola again threw the court into consternation."

Advantage was taken of the short remaining season of dry weather to despatch a lightly-equipped corps of observation in the direction of Tongho, for the purpose of ridding the neighbouring parts of the military bands employed in desolating the country, and driving away both inhabitants and cattle. The British force advanced to Tagoondine, forty miles from Prome, and then the rains setting in, it made for the Irrawaddy, sometimes crossing the path taken by the Burman army in its retreat from Prome. The blighting effects of the Burman system of warfare were here painfully visible. "Even Russia," observes Major Snodgrass, "in her memorable resistance to the armies of Napoleon, did not offer to the invading host such a continued scene of desolation. Neither man nor beast escaped the retiring columns; and heaps of ashes, with groups of hungry, howling dogs, alone indicated where villages had been."

The campaign was now brought to a close, as it was necessary to wait the return of the dry season before resuming operations.

Meanwhile the British army, during the period of their inactivity, were possessed of excellent quarters at Prome, and abundantly supplied with provisions by the people, who, under its protection, again inhabited the surrounding districts.

CHAPTER XXVI.

Burman Head-quarters at Meaday—Shan Female Warriors—Sir A. Campbell makes proposals for Peace to the Burman Monarch—Deputies arrive at the British Camp—An Armistice concluded—The British Commander-in-Chief meets the Burman Chief at Neoung-ben-zeik—The Truce extended to the third of November—Letter of the Kee-Woon-gyee to Sir A. Campbell—Hostilities resumed.

By the end of September the Burman army, recruited from all parts, amounted to seventy thousand men, and the head-quarters were established at Meaday, which place they fortified in the usual manner, digging trenches and building stockades. The Shan contingent amounted to fifteen thousand men, and it was accompanied by three Shan lady warriors of high rank, who promised to deprive the English shot of its destructive power. Sir A. Campbell had, in the early part of the previous August, addressed to the

King of Ava a letter, advising him to listen to the proposals for peace still held out. His Majesty commanded several translations to be made by the English prisoners in Ava; and, when he had fully satisfied himself of the contents, he prepared to open negotiations. Accordingly, two chieftains with attendants arrived at Prome in a war-boat, bearing a flag of truce, on the evening of the 6th of September. These deputies informed the Commander-in-Chief that his letter had been received by their soverign, and his brother was commissioned to treat. They asked for a truce of forty days, and requested that two British officers might return with them to arrange the terms of an armistice. Both these demands obtained the consent of Sir A. Campbell, and he selected as his envoys Lieut.-Colonel Tidy, C.B., Deputy-Adjutant-General, and Lieut. Smith, R.N.

On the morning of the 8th inst. they left with the Burman deputies, who, during their stay in Prome, had taken the opportunity of offering up their prayers in the celebrated pagoda of that city. Arriving at Meaday on the 12th inst. the English officers were conveyed by gilt war-boats to the fort, where they were received with music and military parade.

A cessation of hostilities was agreed on from the date of the armistice to the 17th of October; and further, that on the 2nd of October the first minister of the King should meet the British authorities half-way between the two armies, each party being attended by a guard.

The place chosen for the conference was the village of Neoung-ben-zeik, on the left bank of the Irrawaddy, twenty-five miles above Prome, where a lut'd'hau, or hall of audience, was erected.

Sir A. Campbell's escort comprised one hundred and fifty Governor-General's body-guard dismounted, three hundred and sixty King's troops, as well as Sepoys and artillery, the whole being commanded by Lieut.-Col. Godwin. The Commander-in-Chief and his guard arrived at the rendezvous on the 1st of October. The negotiations were to commence at two o'clock the following day. Two Burman chiefs, chosen for the purpose, conducted Sir A. Campbell to the hall of audience, situated midway between the two camps, which were a thousand yards from each other. Lieut.-col. Tidy and Lieut. Smith escorted the Burman minister to the conference. The British, leaving their camp at the appointed hour, advanced towards the lut'd'hau, the Burman procession commencing its march at the same time.

"Its first appearance," says an eye-witness, "was splendid. It seemed like a moving mass of gold, which, by reflecting the rays of the sun, prevented us at first from distinctly seeing of what it was composed; but, as it advanced, we gradually could perceive, under a canopy of gilt umbrellas, Col. Tidy and Lieut. Smith walking arm-in-arm with two figures dressed in the most gorgeous and extraordinary manner. They were covered with golden ornaments and embroidery, and behind them were fourteen others habited in a similar mode, whilst the rest of the group consisted of followers bearing gilt chattahs, and other paraphernalia of a Burman nobleman. It is impossible to describe the sensations with which we viewed this extraordinary scene. There was something so unexpected in the sudden appearance of this brilliant procession in the midst of these wilds, that, when I gazed at the slow measured pace with which they advanced, and at the supernatural height given to them by their strange apparel, my mind involuntarily recurred to those tales of fiction related of the East, and I could almost have fancied myself an inhabitant of fairy-land, and viewing an assemblage of magicians."

When arrived within a short distance of the hall, Sir A. Campbell advanced to meet the Kee-Woon-gyee. After shaking hands in the English fashion, they proceeded arm-in-arm to the lut'd'hau, where, still following English customs, chairs had been placed. The Kee-Woon-gyee, a good-looking man of about forty years of age, was very observant, and unable to conceal the curiosity and suspicion that lurked beneath a fair exterior. His dress was the full war costume, but his attendants were clothed in the ordinary garments of the country. "One bore his spitting-basin, which was immediately placed by his side, when he seated himself; another held the gold betel and paun boxes, which he now and then presented in a crouching position; and a third carried a gold drinking-cup, richly chased with the twelve signs of the zodiac, and a jar of cold water, wrapped in a plantain-leaf, to keep it cool. The costume of the other chieftains, though very similar in make, was not so highly ornamented as that of the Kee-Woon-gyee." The latter appeared uneasy at the presence of Sir A. Campbell's guard, observing that his own followers were unarmed; so that, to remove all occasion of complaint, the British General dismissed his escort, retaining only the officers of his suite. It was afterwards discovered that this chief, besides his guard of one thousand men, had concealed as many as six thousand in the neighbouring jungle. After a lavish exchange of compliments the Burman Commissioners requested that the present meeting might be considered one of a friendly nature, and that all matters of business might be deferred to the morrow. The Kee-Woon-gyee inquired affectionately after the health of the English King, hoped that friendship might be speedily cemented between the British and Burman nations, and expressed a wish that the officers of the two armies should cultivate each other's acquaintance. Another meeting took place on the following day, at which the terms of peace were discussed. The truce was prolonged to the 3rd of November, that the draft of the treaty might be referred to the King; but at last it became evident that the Burmans had no real intention of accepting the proposed terms, which included indemnification of expenses and a cession of territory. On the 24th of October Sir A. Campbell addressed a letter to the Kee-Woon-gyee, inquiring what was the answer of the Burman court. A reply to this was received on the 29th inst., which removed all further doubt. The letter was written in a somewhat defiant tone, accusing the English of want of faith, and deception. The conclusion of this singular document was as follows:—"If you sincerely want peace, and the re-establishment of our friendship, according to Burman custom, empty your hands of what you have, and then, if you ask it, we will be on friendly terms with you, and forward a petition for the release of the English prisoners, and send them down to you. However, if, after the termination of the armistice between us, you show any inclination to renew your demands for money in payment of your expenses, or any territory from us, you are to consider our friendship at an end. This is Burman custom." The Kee-Woon-gyee, however, was less to blame than his superiors, for he had received peremptory orders to attack the English without delay, and in violation of the armistice; in reply to which he is said to have exclaimed, "No; although it may cost me my life, it is better that one individual should suffer than that the lives of thousands should be lost by such a procedure;" and he kept his word. As soon as the approach of the Burman army became known, the peasantry sought refuge within the British lines, even though obliged to abandon their rice, which was just ready to be gathered in. Prome was in consequence very thickly inhabited. As a precaution against fire, the thatch was taken off the houses—a measure often resorted to in the dry season.

CHAPTER XXVII.

Defeat of the Left Wing of the Burman Army at Sembike—Storming of the Heights of Nepadee—Centre and Right Wing dispersed—The British Army resumes its March ninth of December—Scene at Meaday—The Burmans send in a Flag of Truce—Storming and destruction of Melloon.

ALL hopes of the war being at an end were now extinguished, and it was evident that more blood and treasure would have to be expended before the Burman court could be brought to a sense of its true position. A formidable army of sixty or seventy thousand men advanced to the attack. The right wing, numbering fifteen thousand men, under the command of Sudda-Woon, occupied the right bank of the Irrawaddy, whilst the centre, comprising thirty thousand men, moved down the left or eastern side, led by the Kee-Woon-gyee in person. The left wing, made up chiefly of Shans, and headed by Maha Nemiow, a veteran general of great experience, was fifteen thousand strong, and took up a position at Watty-goon, a village twenty miles north-east of Prome. In addition to these forces, a reserve of ten thousand men, commanded by Prince Memiaboo, occupied Melloon; and a detachment was assembled at Tongho, with the intention of threatening Rangoon.

By the 1st of December the left wing had approached by a slow and cautious movement, stockading and entrenching as it advanced, to Sembike, within a short distance of Prome; and on that day the first action of importance took place.

The troops were formed into two columns, the one commanded by Sir A. Campbell, and the other by General Cotton. To divert the attention of the centre of the Burman army from the meditated attack on the left wing, Sir James Brisbane sailed up the river and cannonaded the heights of Nepadee, where it had taken up a position, strongly fortified.

General Cotton's division arrived first at Sembike, and immediately commenced the assault. The Shans displayed great bravery, opening a well-directed fire, which killed or wounded four officers and sixty men. The contest, however, did not last long; the soldiers forced their way into the crowded works, poured in their volleys, and then with the bayonet quickly drove all before them: the discomfited host flying in the direction of Sir A. Campbell's advancing column, which again dealt destruction on the fugitives. The aged General Memiow was killed while urging on his men; and the two Amazons before mentioned met with that death they seemed to court. One of them is described as "a lovely girl, about seventeen years of age." Her untimely end was greatly lamented by the soldiers, who had so unwillingly caused her death; and they buried her with every mark of respect. Three hundred men, Burmans and Shans, perished in the stockade.

The next day, the 2nd of December, an

advance was made towards the stockaded heights of Nepadee, where, as already stated, the centre of the Burman army had taken up a strong position. A succession of hills rise abruptly from the Irrawaddy, which here is eight hundred yards wide, and on the other side an impenetrable forest afforded a sure protection. The only approach was along a narrow road defended by a battery. The flotilla, under Sir James Brisbane, commenced a sharp cannonade, and the bugles sounded the advance. The 87th Regiment was directed to dislodge a strong body of the enemy, occupying works extending into the jungle, a position it was important for the British troops to gain previous to the main attack. The movement was carried out with great spirit, the men rushing through the jungle and driving the Burmans from their ground. The 38th Regiment, under Colonel Frith, supported by the 13th, now advanced under a heavy fire, and entering the entrenchments speedily gained possession of the works, and pursued the flying foe from height to height. The defeat of the Burman centre was quickly completed. Forty or fifty pieces of artillery were captured, one of which bore the date of the reign of Queen Elizabeth.

The centre and left wing of this great army were now dispersed, but the right wing still occupied stockades on the opposite side of the river. These troops were dislodged on the 15th of December by Brigadier-General Cotton, with a part of his division. By these engagements the Burman army was completely disorganised, sustaining a loss of between two and three thousand men. Most of the Shans retired to their own country, not caring any longer to fight in so desperate a cause.

Immediate obstacles being thus once more removed, the British army was at liberty to resume its march upon Ava. Its total force amounted to forty-five thousand men and twenty-eight pieces of cannon. Two regiments of Native Infantry were left behind at Prome, and the whole of Pegu was placed under the control of British officers.

Sir A. Campbell headed the first division, taking the road to Watty-goon, en route to Meaday, at which place it was supposed the beaten forces of the enemy would rally. Brigadier-General Cotton, commanding the second division, proceeded by the western road, while Brigadier Armstrong, with the Royal Regiment, embarked in the flotilla, under the command of the Commodore, for the general rendezvous at Meaday.

Early on the morning of the 9th of December the first division was on the move. Both men and officers were in high spirits. The latter rode Pegu ponies, and the former were plentifully supplied with provisions. The ponies had been chiefly taken from the defeated Shans. Some of them were sold by auction, when the least valuable fetched from two to three hundred rupees, whilst others were knocked down at eight hundred; and even nine hundred and fifty-six rupees were offered in one instance, a sum equivalent to £95 12*s*. British money. This value was merely temporary, and three months later the same animals did not realise a fourth part of their original price.

The distance from Prome to Ava, the march now contemplated by the British troops, is by land about three hundred miles, and all were curious to behold the beauties and wonders of the golden city.

On the 19th instant, after a trying march, during which the men suffered much from heavy rains, they arrived at Meaday. The place was found to be evacuated, and, says Major Snodgrass in his journal, "A scene of misery and death awaited us. Within and around the stockades, the ground was strewed with dead and dying, lying promiscuously together, the victims of disease and want. Here and there a small white pagoda marked where a man of rank lay buried, while numerous new-made graves plainly denoted that what we saw was merely the small remnant of mortality which the hurried departure of the enemy had prevented them from burying. The beach and neighbouring jungles were filled with dogs and vultures, whose growling and screaming, added to the pestilential smell of the place, rendered our situation far from pleasant. Here and there a faithful dog might be seen stretched out and moaning over a new-made grave, or watching by the side of his still-breathing master; but by far the greater number, deprived of the hand that fed them, went prowling with the vultures among the dead, or lay upon the ground glutted with their foul repast. As if this scene of death had not sufficed, fresh horrors were added to it by the sanguinary leaders of these unhappy men. Several gibbets were found erected about the stockades, each bearing the mouldering remains of three or four crucified victims, thus cruelly put to death—for, perhaps, no greater crime than that of wandering from their post in search of food, or, at the very worst, for having followed the example of their chiefs in flying from the enemy."

The next day the army hastened to depart, and pushed on through a depopulated country towards Melloon. And now a flag of truce was sent by the Burmans to meet the advancing force, as a Commissioner named Kolein Menghie had arrived with full powers from the king to conclude a treaty of peace. The army advanced to a town opposite Melloon named Patanagoh, and on the 1st of January, 1826, the first meeting of the Commissioners took place, in a large accommodation boat, moored by the Burmans in the middle of the Irrawaddy. After four meetings, and long discussions, the terms were at length accepted, fifteen days being allowed for obtaining the king's ratification, the delivery of prisoners, and the payment of the first instalment of money. The Burmans, however, again trifled, and the negotiations terminated as before in hostilities being resumed. On the 19th of January operations commenced, at 11 o'clock A.M., against Melloon. Batteries had been thrown up and heavy ordnance landed. A heavy fire was now opened, and the troops, divided into four columns, embarked in the flotilla. Having effected a landing, the men moved forward to the attack with their wonted bravery. The ladders were placed and the walls scaled in a very short space of time, the Burmans retreating in dense columns before the little band of soldiers who had so soon possessed themselves of works deemed impregnable by the Burman generals.

Fifteen thousand men were driven out of Melloon, and vast military stores fell into the hands of the victors, including seventy-nine pieces of cannon, twenty tons of gunpowder, seventeen hundred muskets, large quantities of grain, and documents which sufficiently proved the perfidy of the chiefs. Amongst these was the treaty which it was pretended had been sent to Ava for the king's ratification, so that the whole proceeding was proved to have been a deception; though it is not so easy to see the object they had in view, for the armistice was of greater service to the advancing troops, exhausted as they were by marching and sickness, than to themselves.

Mrs. Judson remarks very truly of this

people, "They have no idea either of moral excellence or the utility of good faith. They would consider it nothing less than folly to keep a treaty when they could gain anything by breaking it. The fidelity hitherto observed by the British Government in fulfilling the stipulations of the late treaty stupified the Burmans. They knew not what to make of it. I heard many use expressions like the following: 'The Kulas, although they drink spirits and slay cattle, and are ambitious and rapacious, have a regard for truth and their word which is quite extraordinary, whereas in us Burmans there is no truth.'"

As soon as the wounded had been removed to a place of safety, and the military stores secured, the works were set on fire, producing a magnificent illumination, and this stronghold was reduced to ashes.

CHAPTER XXVIII.

The British Forces push onwards—Arrival of Doctors Price and Sandford with a message from the Burman King—He accepts the services of the "King of Hell"—Defeat of his Troops at Pagan Mew—The British Army encamps at Yandaboo—Ratification of the Treaty of Peace—Terms of the Treaty—Court Historian's account of the War—War of 1852—Conclusion.

THE capture of Melloon having been thus so successfully achieved, the British forces, on the 25th of June, resumed their onward progress. The road now lay through a hilly country of much poorer soil than the plains of Pegu, and dotted with shrubs or trees of stunted growth. "After marching six miles," says one who accompanied the expedition, "we reached the summit of a steep hill, which commanded a magnificent view of the surrounding country. A large plain lay beneath us covered with wood and ornamented with numerous pagodas, some of great antiquity, bespeaking the grandeur or opulence of what had been, in days of yore, a considerable town; whilst two or three of later date, and neatly whitewashed, indicated that religion had not been neglected by the inhabitants of the little hamlets of Taimboop and Meingoon. In the valley on our left rolled the Irrawaddy, whose course might be traced for many miles, and on its opposite bank ran two or three ridges of hills, here and there crowned with pagodas, and gradually merging into the distant Arracan mountains, which were but faintly visible in the horizon."

On the 31st of June the advancing columns encamped in the neighbourhood of the petroleum wells, and hopes of a speedy termination of the war were excited by the arrival of Dr. Sandford of the Royals (who had some time previously been taken prisoner), Dr. Price, an American missionary, and four liberated prisoners of war. Drs. Sandford and Price were on their parole, and had been deputed by the king to convey a message to the British general. The appearance of these gentlemen was singularly grotesque and Crusoe-like; their hair and beards were of great length, and their clothes were made of Tartan cloth. His Burman majesty was anxious to learn the most lenient terms on which he might conclude a peace. These were fully explained, and on the next day the two deputies set out for Ava in the confident hope that war was now virtually at an end; but on their arrival in the city they found that a great change had taken place in the disposition of the Burman court. The king had again listened to evil councillors. An officer at court had volunteered his services, undertaking with thirty thousand men to drive away the audacious strangers, and vindicate the honour of the Burman arms. His offer was eagerly accepted, and the title of "Nai-woon-Barein," or "King of Hell," was bestowed upon him. The patriotism, pride, and cupidity of the people were appealed to, large bounties were given, and the recruits received the honourable appellation of "Retrievers of the King's Glory." Nai-woon-Barein assembled his forces at Pagan-Mew, and on the 8th of February prepared to make good his word. Eight thousand men were stationed within the city walls, whilst the Burman general advanced with the rest of his troops, from sixteen to twenty thousand in number, to meet the British forces, which numbered less than two thousand fighting-men, the 47th and 87th regiments not having reached the spot. An engagement quickly ensued, which speedily ended in the entire defeat and dispersion of this last hope of the Burman king. The sentence of Nai-woon-Barein, or the King of Hell, was death by command of the King. The road to the capital was now entirely open and unobstructed, and the whole country lay at the mercy of the invader.

Here terminated, after the expenditure of much blood and treasure, this first war of the British with the Burman nation. Whilst the danger was at a distance the king cared little how many of his subject-slaves were sacrificed to his infatuation and flung at the British cannon as food for powder, but the steady advance of the foe towards his capital made him tremble for his personal safety and the security of his throne.

Accordingly, Doctors Price and Sandford, accompanied by Mr. Judson, were despatched in all haste to the British camp to announce the submission of the king, and his acceptance of the terms proposed: but the request was made that six lacs of rupees might be accepted till the invading army should have retired to Prome, when the other nineteen would be paid. The Burman monarch, judging by what his own policy would be, feared that after the money had been advanced the British General would still take possession of Ava, and refuse the terms he previously agreed upon. Such a proposition, however, was not listened to; and the king was further informed that, if the terms now offered were not accepted and the treaty ratified within five hours, much greater concessions would be insisted on; in the interim the British forces would still continue their advance to the capital. Messrs. Judson and Price hastened to convey this ultimatum to the Burman monarch, and on the 22nd of February the army encamped at Yandaboo, within forty-five miles, or three marches, of Ava. Soon after a war-boat was observed approaching, and, as it neared the anxious spectators, Messrs. Judson and Price and some other liberated prisoners were recognised. During the war Mrs. Judson, who had adopted the Burman costume for prudential reasons, remained at large and administered to the wants of her husband. Dr. Price was able to announce to Sir A. Campbell the acceptance by the Burman government of all the terms of the treaty. Boats shortly afterwards arrived bearing the first instalment, viz. twenty-five lacs of rupees, or £250,000, and two ministers of state vested with full powers to conclude and ratify the terms imposed by the British General. The bullion that made up the required amount was of the most miscellaneous description, and had evidently been wrung from the people. There were cups of gold and silver, gold chains of nobility, and coins of different nations; to these were added a few bars of gold from the royal treasury. The commissioners presented their credentials to Sir A. Campbell, while the royal mandate was produced and carefully opened. A small red velvet bag, bound with tape, and sealed with the royal signet, inclosed a cylindrical case made of ivory, in which was a small bag of gold cloth. When this was opened, a second of the same costly material, wrapped with cotton, appeared, and in this was the royal order written on a small piece of vellum paper, with a flowered gold border, and purporting that the Woongyee and A-twen-woon were directed to proceed to the British camp, and arrange all subjects of dispute, to the satisfaction of the British commissioners. To this no signature was attached, such not being customary; but the paper was declared by Messrs. Judson and Price perfectly satisfactory; and, the articles of the treaty being then separately read, the Burmans acquiesced in every one without demurring in the least. They also engaged themselves to procure boats sufficient for the transportation of five thousand men to Rangoon, and agreed to indemnify the prisoners for all their losses within five days.*

On the 24th of February, 1826, the treaty of Yandaboo was formally signed and sealed, a royal salute announcing to the troops that peace was at last concluded. The terms agreed to may be briefly stated as follows:

1st. That the Burman monarch cedes to the British the Tenasserim provinces, Arracan, and a part of Martaban.

2nd. That the king of Ava relinquishes all claim to the states of Cachar, Jyntea, and Assam.

3rd. That Munipore shall be declared independent and under British protection.

4th. The reception of a British resident at Ava. The privilege to be mutual.

* "Two Years in Ava."

5th. The negotiation of a commercial treaty.

6th. The payment of one crore of rupees (one million pounds sterling) towards the expenses of the war. Twenty-five lacs to be handed over to the British authorities before the army should leave the country, and the remainder in three separate instalments; the last to be paid within two years from the date of the treaty.

Burman arrogance and ambition were thus humbled and checked at least for a time. Their largest armies and bravest generals had been sent in vain against the white strangers. The haughty Bandoola, and the charmed "Invulnerables", the fierce "King of Hell," and the "Retrievers of the King's Glory" had all equally failed, and either fallen bravely in the field or fled before the charge of the British bayonet.

The account of this war recorded in the national chronicles by the court historian was as follows: "In the years 1186 and 87 the Kalu-pyu, or white strangers of the west, fastened a quarrel upon the Lord of the Golden Palace. They landed at Rangoon, took that place and Prome, and were permitted to advance as far as Yandaboo; for the king, from motives of piety and regard to life, made no effort whatever to oppose them. The strangers had spent vast sums of money in their enterprise; and by the time they reached Yandaboo their resources were exhausted, and they were in great distress. They petitioned the king, who in his clemency and generosity sent them large sums of money to pay expenses, and ordered them out of the country."

Twenty-six years from the date of the treaty of Yandaboo brings us to 1852, when a second struggle with the Burman nation took place. This war would appear to have had its origin in comparatively trifling causes, and those ignorant of Indian affairs, and the people with whom the Anglo-Indian government had to deal, found great room for animadversion. The Burman governor of Rangoon, besides oppressing British subjects there, commenced a system of extortion on the commanders of British merchant-ships trading to that port; as was particularly exemplified in the cases of Messrs. Sheppard and Lewis. These outrages being laid before the supreme government at Calcutta, a force was despatched to settle matters, amicably if possible, with the Burman government. In this crisis, in the event of the contumacy of the King of Ava, war was the only means of redress. The Burman monarch chose that alternative, and the struggle, which presents nothing remarkable, will still be fresh in the recollection of the British public. It ended in the seizure, rather than the cession, of Pegu and the province of Martaban; the British authorities rightly judging that any treaty with the Burmans is not worth the paper on which it is written.

Although the terrible events of last year will, with much reason, strengthen the feeling of opposition to the extension of our territories in the East, yet it is hardly possible to avoid the conclusion that the whole of Burmah must finally be subjected to British rule. On reviewing the history of British dominion in the East, it will appear that our Indian empire—from the time that Clive laid deep its foundations on the ruins of the Mogul monarchy, and his successors reared the splendid superstructure, to the present day, when British influence extends from the slopes of the Himmalaya to Cape Comorin, from the Indus to the borders of Siam—seems ever to have held expansion of frontier as the law of its existence. The red line, indicative of British sway, is ever pushing forward, knocking over crazy governments and tottering thrones; sparing neither golden monarchs nor any other titled imbecility. It crosses the widest rivers, leaps over the highest mountains, and encircles countries of which our forefathers possessed but the dimmest possible intimation; and, however desirable it may be to consolidate rather than extend, to improve rather than conquer—yet it is to be feared to stop while aught remains to oppose would be the first step towards retrogression; and we can only hope, that in process of time, when British civilization, so slow to take root in that eastern soil, shall have gradually extended itself, and Christianity shall have infused somewhat of its own spirit into the native mind, greatness of extent will not be so antagonistic to union and strength, that the march of improvement will begin in real earnest, and our vast Indian possessions attain to as great a degree of prosperity as the other parts of the British Empire.

APPENDIX.

TABLE of the FALL OF RAIN at TAVOY during SIX YEARS, by DR. MORTON.

1841.		1842.		1843.	
May . . .	29·1	May . . .	30·6	May . . .	7·7
June . .	66·5	June . .	46·9	June . .	61·4
July . . .	60·4	July . . .	70·3	July . . .	44·9
August . .	26·9	August . .	35·3	August . .	39·6
September .	50·2	September .	42·1	September .	30·6
October .	5·7	October .	5·2	October .	4·9
November .	1·6	November .	0·3	November .	1·5
	240·4		230·7		190·6

1844.		1845.		1846.	
May . . .	18·0	May . . .	29·0	May . . .	16·8
June . .	42·5	June . .	49·9	June . .	48·9
July . . .	36·9	July . . .	51·0	July . . .	47·7
August . .	32·0	August . .	46·3	August . .	60·0
September .	25·2	September .	32·2	September .	45·1
October .	14·0	October .	18·8	October .	8·8
November .	6·6	November .	2·4	November .	3·9
	175·2		229·6		231·2

LIST of IMPORTS and EXPORTS in TAVOY

ARTICLES.	With Customs.						Free of		
	Imports.			Exports.			Imports.		
	R.	A.	P.	R.	A.	P.	R.	A.	P.
Betelnuts	1,283	2	2	..	..		322	8	0
Cardamums	..	..		480	0	0	10	0	0
Cocoa-nuts	4,256	3	0	..	..		181	0	0
Cotton, Raw	..	..		..	..		6,050	3	0
Ditto, Manufactures	5,295	8	4	43	8	0	5,324	12	0
Crockeryware	736	6	0	..	..		12	6	0
Cutlery and Hardware	1,332	14	0	42	0	0	753	12	0
Dammer	21	12	9	..	..		1,014	0	0
Dannee Leaves	..	..		..	..		37	0	0
Earthenware	13	4	0	44	4	0	5,209	8	0
Fish of all sorts	..	..		220	0	0	7,363	4	0
Fruits and Preserves	..	..		..	..		47	0	0
Garlic and Onions	10	0	0	..	..		1,569	0	0
Glassware	247	6	0	..	..		51	0	0
Iron and Steel	1,018	14	10	..	..		290	0	0
Jagry	..	..		..	..		718	0	0
Lackered ware	..	..		9	8	0	4,980	0	0
Oil	526	2	0	..	..		826	0	0
Rattans	..	..		..	..		2,808	4	0
Rice and Paddy	..	..		149,380	15	4	1,631	12	0
Salt	..	..		..	..		..	..	
Silk, Raw	450	0	0	..	..		108	0	0
Ditto, Manufactures	14	12	0	7	8	0	2,850	0	0
Timber and Boards	..	..		..	..		442	8	0
Tea	641	12	0	..	..		61	12	9
Tin	..	..		200	0	0	15	0	0
Tobacco	60	7	0	36	8	0	19,016	12	0
Torches	..	..		12	0	0	3,742	0	0
Twist and Thread	4,140	8	0	..	..		1,622	0	0
Wine and Spirits	103	12	0	..	..		..	..	
Sundry Articles of Manufactures	2,920	15	2	36	10	0	4,571	11	0
Ditto Food	762	0	0	3	2	0	6,081	6	0
Sundries not enumerated in the above	..	..		2	0	0	10,077	8	0
Total Value of Articles	23,835	11	3	150,517	15	4	87,787	14	9
Total Treasure	..	..		..	..		123,224	0	0
Total Value and Treasure	23,835	11	3	150,517	15	4	211,011	14	9

[For an account of the RECEIPTS and DISBURSEMENTS

during the Year 1856–57, with their Values.

Customs.	Total Value of Articles with Customs and Free of Customs.		Retained in the Province.	Re-exported from the Province.
Exports.	Imports.	Exports.		
R. A. P.	R. A. P.	R. A. P.	R. A. P.	R. A. P.
1,973 12 0	1,605 10 2	1,973 12 0	.. ..	368 1 10
1,517 12 0	10 0 0	1,997 12 0	.. ..	1,987 12 0
1,903 0 0	4,437 3 0	1,903 0 0	2,534 3 0	
469 0 0	6,050 3 0	469 0 0	5,581 3 0	
1,692 7 0	10,620 4 4	1,735 15 0	8,884 5 4	
519 4 0	748 12 0	519 4 0	229 8 0	
192 8 0	2,080 10 0	234 8 0	1,852 2 0	
.. ..	1,035 12 9	.. ..	1,035 12 9	
10,107 0 0	37 0 0	10,107 0 0	.. ..	10,070 0 0
2,091 13 0	5,222 12 0	2,136 1 0	3,086 11 0	
9,487 4 0	7,363 4 0	9,707 4 0	.. ..	1,711 0 0
10,119 10 0	47 0 0	10,119 10 0	.. ..	10,072 10 0
107 12 0	1,579 0 0	107 12 0	1,471 4 0	
.. ..	298 6 0	.. ..	298 6 0	
338 0 0	1,308 14 10	338 0 0	970 14 10	
20,334 2 0	718 0 0	20,334 2 0	.. ..	19,616 2 0
91 0 0	4,980 0 0	100 8 0	4,879 8 0	
523 0 0	1,352 2 0	523 0 0	829 2 0	
2,023 0 0	2,808 4 0	2,023 0 0	785 0 0	
4,001 0 0	1,631 12 0	153,381 15 4	.. ..	151,750 3 4
4,995 6 0	.. ..	4,995 6 0	.. ..	4,995 6 0
173 0 0	558 0 0	173 0 0	385 0 0	
1,258 0 0	2,864 12 0	1,265 8 0	1,599 4 0	
3,187 0 0	442 8 0	3,187 0 0	.. ..	2,744 8 0
781 0 0	703 8 9	781 0 0	.. ..	77 7 3
155 0 0	15 0 0	355 0 0	.. ..	340 0 0
2,686 11 0	19,077 3 0	2,723 3 0	16,354 0 0	
1,796 0 0	3,742 0 0	1,808 0 0	1,934 0 0	
569 0 0	5,762 8 0	569 0 0	5,193 8 0	
70 0 0	103 12 0	70 0 0	33 12 0	
4,869 10 0	7,492 10 2	4,906 4 0	2,586 6 2	
1,032 5 0	6,843 6 0	1,035 7 0	5,807 15 0	
799 14 0	10,077 8 0	801 14 0	9,275 10 0	
89,864 2 0	111,623 10 0	240,382 1 4	75,607 7 1	203,733 2 5
800 0 0	123,224 0 0	800 0 0	122,424 0 0	
90,664 2 0	234,847 10 0	241,182 1 4	198,031 7 1	203,733 2 5

of the PROVINCE of TAVOY, see last page.]

GENERAL STATEMENT of the REVENUE of the TENASSERIM PROVINCES
REMAINING UNCOLLECTED

Districts.	Articles.	For 1853-4.					
		R.	A.	P.	R.	A.	P.
Amherst .	Paddy land . .	132,567	7	1			
Tavoy . .	Ditto . . .	48,309	13	6			
Mergui .	Ditto . . .	19,012	3	5	199,889	8	0
Amherst .	Garden land . .	31,738	1	7			
Tavoy . .	Ditto . . .	17,503	8	4			
Mergui .	Ditto . . .	8,543	9	10	57,785	3	9
Amherst .	Capitation tax . .	34,195	0	0			
Tavoy . .	Ditto . . .	10,170	0	0			
Mergui .	Ditto . . .	9,793	0	0	54,158	0	0
Amherst .	Salt tax . . .	2,194	4	0			
Tavoy . .	Ditto . . .	1,271	10	0			
Mergui .	Ditto . . .	0	0	0	3,465	14	0
Amherst .	Timber revenue .	96,114	10	6			
Tavoy . .	Ditto . . .	0	0	0			
Mergui .	Ditto . . .	0	0	0	96,114	10	6
Amherst .	Sayer revenue . .	74,344	1	0			
Tavoy . .	Ditto . . .	7,458	0	0			
Mergui .	Ditto . . .	9,609	0	0	91,501	1	0
Amherst .	Marine receipts. .	48,918	4	2			
Tavoy . .	Ditto . . .	142	10	0			
Mergui .	Ditto . . .	262	0	0	49,322	14	2
Amherst .	Judicial receipts .	48,872	1	1			
Tavoy . .	Ditto . . .	6,712	7	2			
Mergui .	Ditto . . .	5,621	4	8	61,205	12	11
Amherst .	Bazaar rent . .	0	0	0			
Tavoy .	Ditto . . .	1,926	0	0			
Mergui .	Ditto . . .	2,138	1	10	4,064	1	10
Amherst .	Postage and postage stamps . . .	2,248	0	8			
Tavoy . .	Ditto . . .	11	8	4			
Mergui .	Ditto . . .	91	14	11	2,351	7	11
Amherst .	Birds'-nests Farm .	0	0	0			
Tavoy . .	Ditto . . .	7,170	0	0			
Mergui .	Ditto . . .	3,200	0	0	10,370	0	0
Amherst .	Miscellaneous receipts	1,285	6	1			
Tavoy . .	Ditto . . .	418	13	2			
Mergui .	Ditto . . .	367	11	7	2,071	14	10
		Total Co.'s rupees .			632,300	8	11

for the YEARS 1853–54, 1854–55, and 1855–56, and the BALANCE on the 1st MAY, 1856.

For 1854-55.						For 1855-56.					
R.	A.	P.	R.	A.	P.	R.	A.	P.	R.	A.	P.
129,856	0	7				127,777	1	3			
51,884	15	9				51,012	15	10			
17,823	1	9	199,564	2	1	18,964	12	9	197,754	13	10
30,654	4	9				30,660	8	6			
15,856	8	6				15,906	1	4			
8,393	2	0	54,903	15	3	8,350	3	7	54,916	13	5
35,332	0	0				36,342	0	0			
10,550	0	0				11,142	0	0			
9,843	0	0	55,725	0	0	9,688	0	0	57,172	0	0
3,596	4	0				2,468	8	0			
1,259	4	0				1,062	14	0			
0	0	0	4,855	8	0	0	0	0	3,531	6	0
138,461	13	2				172,290	3	11			
0	0	0				0	0	0			
0	0	0	138,461	13	2	0	0	0	172,290	3	11
95,495	5	3				114,808	14	4			
7,656	4	0				8,602	0	0			
8,857	7	3	112,009	0	6	12,094	12	1	135,505	10	5
35,588	10	10				11,495	2	8			
548	7	1				332	4	8			
340	0	0	36,477	1	11	263	5	6	12,090	12	10
50,319	14	8				55,242	9	4			
12,238	1	4				11,828	9	6½			
6,663	3	2	69,161	3	2	6,454	5	0	73,525	7	10½
0	0	6				0	0	0			
1,944	0	0				2,022	0	0			
2,345	12	1	4,289	12	1	2,076	0	0	4,098	0	0
5,162	13	11				8,933	3	1			
120	6	6				226	10	6			
234	13	11	5,518	2	4	72	3	10	9,232	1	5
0	0	0				0	0	0			
3,600	0	0				3,600	0	0			
3,200	0	0	6,800	0	0	2,310	0	0	5,910	0	0
40,145	5	3				73,128	6	7			
1,279	15	9				5,998	4	6			
1,686	1	4	43,111	6	4	1,336	2	5	80,462	13	6
			730,877	0	10				806,490	3	2¼

The Revenues of the Province of TAVOY have steadily increased under the British rule. The entire collections in 1838, the first year of which complete record is found, were Rs. 94,416, against an expenditure of Rs. 93,348.

For the year ending 30th of April, 1857, the Receipts and Disbursements were as follows:—

RECEIPTS.

	R.	A.	P.
Wet Lands	52,214	4	3
Up Lands	2,962	1	0
Gardens	12,561	5	3
Capitation Tax	11,506	0	0
Government Bazaar	2,446	0	0
Edible Bird-nest Monopoly	3,600	0	0
Tax on Manufacture of Salt	512	12	0
Monopoly of Sale of Spirituous Liquors	4,134	0	0
Opium	7,409	0	0
Judicial Receipts	11,919	7	5
Sea Customs	5,851	0	8
Post Office	218	8	0
Total	115,334	6	7

DISBURSEMENTS.

		R.	A.	P.	R.	A.	P.
1. Revenue	Establishment	10,260	7	10½			
"	Contingencies	8,441	6	2			
					18,701	14	0½
"	Sea Customs Establishment	...	...		786	14	0
"	Post Office	...	...		182	11	0
"	Cost of Opium	...	...		2,007	8	0
2. Judicial	Establishment	29,047	1	2½			
"	Pension	367	8	0			
"	Contingencies	21,255	10	0			
					50,670	3	2½
3. General	Educational Grant in aid	300	0	0			
"	Medical Establishment	2,100	0	0			
"	Contingencies	1,039	2	5			
					3,439	2	5
4. Marine	Establishment	585	0	0			
"	Pensions	333	0	0			
"	Contingencies	1,941	13	1			
					2,859	13	1
5. Military	Establishment	10,663	4	0			
"	Contingencies	327	15	0			
					10,991	3	0
	Total				89,639	4	9